THE TRUE STORY OF
THE NOTORIOUS JESSE JAMES

THE
TRUE STORY
OF THE
NOTORIOUS
JESSE JAMES

EVANS NEWMANS

427076

An Exposition-Lochinvar Book

EXPOSITION PRESS   HICKSVILLE, NEW YORK

FIRST EDITION

© 1976 by Evans Newmans
Copyright © under the Universal Copyright and Berne
Conventions

ISBN 0-682-48534-9

Printed in the United States of America

PROLOGUE

Those who knew him said Jesse James was a good boy. That is simple fact. In boyhood, both Jesse and his brother Frank were notably fond of animals. In the case of Jesse, this tenderness toward dumb beasts continued until the day of his death. When Jesse James, stricken by an assassin's bullet, lay dead upon the floor of his home, a small dog was one of his chief mourners, and his grief showed plainly. Ten days earlier, the dog had been given to Jesse by his half-sister, at the home of their mother. The trip from there required a ride of two days on horseback. Jesse James carried the little dog in his arms all the way.

Frank and Jesse James, according to their neighbors, were just like other boys. They were neither more devilish nor more saintly than the average American lad who grows up in a rural community. They were healthy, hearty youngsters. They played like other farm boys everywhere; they romped and they wrestled. They went swimming in the creek nearby, in the summer. They built snow forts and were fair marksmen as snow-ballers in the winter. They fought in earnest, as the other fellows did, when a playmate became aggressive or when they themselves picked fights and went after the other fellows. There was nothing whatsoever in their small-boy careers to set them apart from millions of other lads growing up on American farms just before the outbreak of the Civil War—that is to say, nothing from the inside out. From the outside in, there was much that made their early experiences and impressions different from those of other boys in other sections of the United States.

It is to be emphasized that, on the Missouri-Kansas border, the war had already begun—about seven years before the South Carolinians fired upon Fort Sumter. From approximately 1854 to 1861, western Missouri and eastern Kansas were fighting each other with a ferocity and a fatality hard to describe to the present generation.

The border was a realm beyond the law. Although it was not a vast geographical area, its effect and influence were great, not only upon the abolitionist movement in the North, but also upon the secessionist movement in the South. It was only natural that Missouri and Kansas fight each other, Kansas being inhabited by Northerners, many of them from New England, and Missouri, along the western border, having been settled by Southerners from Kentucky, Tennessee, Virginia, and other slave states. Free-soil Kansas settlers invaded the border counties of Missouri and carried off slaves. Slaveholding Missourians, and many Missourians of the Border-Ruffian type, who owned no slaves but believed in the institution of slavery, invaded Kansas territory and voted illegally, hoping to make Kansas a slave state. Kansas Jayhawkers and Red-Legs, Missouri Border Ruffians and Bushwhackers—even the groups' names are suggestive.

When Emerson's "sublime fanatic," John Brown, of Osawatomie, set himself the insuperable one-man task of eradicating slavery, and beginning specifically in Kansas Territory, the border warfare was already well under way. John Brown was by no means the only man along the border who believed himself to be above the law. There were thousands of others, in Missouri and Kansas, who, from whatever motives, had placed themselves upon platforms of opinion and activity so far above the law that they could see neither the American Constitution nor statutes of state or territory.

Hell on earth broke loose along the border. In time, the fight lost its dignity. No longer a direct issue between freedom and slavery, it became a vulgar, vicious, and vain conflict, man-to-man, hand-to-hand, exhibiting the basest human passions. On both sides of the border were men who made the warfare a matter of immediate personal interest—as they conceived it. Kansans entered Missouri, seized slaves, and sold them back for ransom. Missourians went into Kansas and killed Kansans who had seized, or were supposedly intending to seize, slaves.

Kansans, on the pretext of liberating Negroes, invaded Missouri and stole horses, cattle, hogs, even chickens, carrying their loot to Kansas. Missourians retaliated in kind, but with a lesser measure of success. Both sides were without scruples.

Kansans and Missourians ambushed and shot each other. Missourians and Kansans hanged each other from trees or from barn rafters. Robbery and murder were so frequent on both sides of the line that such crimes lost their sensationalism and became well-nigh commonplace events.

Enter now, by your leave, the two little Jameses. Alexander Franklin, known to outlaw history as Frank, was hardly eleven years old when the border war began; he was born January 10, 1843. Jesse Woodson, Frank's little brother, was about seven, having begun his unique career on September 5, 1847.

THE TRUE STORY OF
THE NOTORIOUS JESSE JAMES

1

Jesse James was born on an old homestead three or four miles from the small village of Centerville, now Kearney. Frank's birthplace was a cabin-like domicile about three miles away.

The parents of the James boys were from Kentucky. Both had come from sturdy pioneer families whose forebears had traversed the old Wilderness Road on the long trek which had resulted in the winning of the earlier West. Logan County was the Kentucky center of the Jameses.

The Coles, Jesse's mother's family, settled at and near Lexington, in the bluegrass region. Miss Zerelda Cole had a mind of her own. Having come from a convent at Lexington, she married James, Baptist minister, not permitting religion to interfere with love. For that matter, love became her religion. In time, although the element of hate entered and nearly destroyed her little heaven on earth, her love never waned; it increased in its intensity year after year, until the end.

After having lived for about ten years in Missouri and cultivating his farm by working hard between Sundays, the young Reverend James made up his mind to go to the California goldfields to try to acquire enough wealth to educate his growing family. He had gotten almost nothing from his labors in the Master's vineyard. There were three children. Susie had followed Jesse into the world, after an interval of about two years.

Jesse was not quite four when his father was ready to start the long trip overland. The child clung to his father.

"Don't go, Pa; please don't go away and leave us!"

Jesse pleaded, his tears falling. The Reverend Mr. James looked at his wife, and she, at him. For a moment, both were silent.

"Zerelda," he said, at last, "if I hadn't promised those other men I'd go with them, and hadn't gone to so much expense

11

already, I'd surely stay at home. Poor little Jesse—he needs me. But you have the Negroes to help you, and I reckon I ought not to back out now."

Little Jesse still clung, still pleaded.

"It's all right, Jesse," said his father. "I'll come back home with lots of money and send you and Frank through college, and maybe you'll grow up to be great and good men. You'll have a better start than your father had, anyhow."

He set Jesse down, said good-bye to all, climbed to the seat of his covered wagon, and set his course resolutely toward the Far West. They never saw him again. The caravan reached California and the gold region nearly four months later. Less than three weeks after the journey's end came the final journey's end for the Reverend Robert James—he took sick and died. Many years afterward, his two outlaw sons visited Maryville, California, where he was supposed to have been buried, but they never found his grave.

Tragedy first entered the old homestead when the news came from California.

The young widow took another husband a couple of years later, but divorced him because he was unkind to Frank and Jesse. Dr. Samuel, her third and last spouse, fulfilled all requirements; he stood by "the boys" until Jesse was slain and Frank "came in," stood trial, was acquitted, and settled down to good citizenship. Like the Reverend Mr. James, he was a Kentuckian from an old family.

Frank James was a good enough boy. Local history has it that Frank as a little fellow was just as good a boy as his younger brother was until he was about fifteen but, as Frank got into his late teens, he got to be "a little wild." Frank, being nearly five years older than Jesse, was that much farther along toward maturity throughout the border-war era. Frank probably took into his soul somewhat more of the blood and iron of those years, which may account in part for his wildness. A big boy in the midst of a lot of shooting and looting will take it all more seriously than does a smaller boy.

Frank James, throughout adult life, was a serious-minded

man. Jesse was virtually the reverse. Frank "took things seriously"; Jesse took things more light-heartedly. Frank was by nature
morose, Jesse, constitutionally cheerful. Frank was for thinking
out a proposition, Jesse, for going at it on the instant's edge.
Frank counseled moderation; Jesse was inclined to radical action.

Just here may be the very place for suggesting that, if these
two brothers, as outlaws, had been alike as two green peas,
and Frank, like Jesse, rather than the other way about, their
period of outlawry in all probability would have been punctuated
by a pair of bullets—long before it attained its world-beating
record of sixteen years.

Life was by no means all play for the Jameses when they
were boys. They were brought up to work, and work hard.
On a Missouri farm a century ago, such things as labor-
saving devices were unknown. Farm work meant real work,
sweat-o'-the-brow toil, back-wearying labor. From the time they
were big enough to drive a horse and hold the handles of a plow,
Frank and Jesse were "hands" on the old home farm. They
planted, hoed, plowed, harvested. Wheat, corn, hay, garden
truck—all were grown there. Horses to feed and curry, cows to
care for and milk, hogs to call and corral, firewood to chop
and split—the chores alone were enough, winter or summer,
to keep the two growing lads in healthful exercise.

The hard work had its compensations. The open air and the
physical effort gave the boys good health and hearty appetites.
There was always plenty of wholesome food on the table. The
mother of the Jameses, in addition to her old-time religion, had
the old-fashioned notion that good cooking is necessary to the
conservation of good food. She was a capable cook, of the
Kentucky pioneer persuasion.

I have already alluded to the border warfare having altered
the boys' environment from that of boys in, let us say,
New London County, Connecticut, or Albermarle County,
Virginia. They dwelt but a few miles north of the Missouri
River. Immediately south of that river, and of Clay County, lies
Jackson County, the center of before-the-war riding, raiding,
robbing, and raping in Missouri. Much of this deviltry had

roots also in Clay County. What the James lads didn't see or hear, they heard about. The grownups, seated on the front porch in summertime or before the blazing fireplace in winter, talked it all over in presence of the children. Discussions of opinion were well-nigh as violent as some of the desperate deeds under discussion.

So it happened that the Jameses and their playmates, instead of continuing to play the old-time game called town ball, precursor of the sport that made Walter Johnson famous, also engaged in games of grimmer and ghastlier genre. They played, whenever they could induce some boy to stand for the chief character, "Old Jim Lane" or "Old John Brown." Neither John Brown nor General Lane was old, as we estimate age today; but the word in those times indicated that he whose name it preceded was ancient in sin and crime and all manner of iniquity.

Missouri border men and women hated Brown and Lane, to whom they ascribed in their fury many of their miseries. Boyhood on the Missouri border most naturally shared this feeling. It was difficult to find any boy who would undergo the ignominy of playing the character of Jim Lane or John Brown. However, boys who sought the ecstasy and honor of shooting or hanging Brown or Lane—in play, mind you—were able to obtain raw material for those characters by agreeing to reverse the roles and themselves submit to the disgrace the next time they played the exciting and satisfying game. Thus it came about that General Lane, the "Grim Liberator," was shot or drowned or hanged many times over in Missouri, by boys who resented his Free-Soil activities. And all this was many years before he poked the muzzle of a revolver into his own mouth and killed himself, an about-to-be-disgraced United States senator. That was some years before John Brown was hanged in Virginia for his so-called treason to that state, but the border boys had shot him, too, full of holes or stretched his neck many times beneath many an overhanging limb. Raiding and robbing were only incidental to these executions all done in play and yet not without violent feelings.

Should you seek seriously for the germ of all-around outlawry in Missouri, invented and carried on by border men in the Roaring Forties reared there in the Rip-roaring Fifties, ignore not those seven years preceding Sumter.

Frank James had turned eighteen when North and South finally clashed in arms. He was old enough and big enough to go into the army—a tall, sinewy, nervy fellow. Already he possessed two essential military qualifications; he could ride hard and shoot straight. There was a story told that, when Frank and Jesse were big enough to share the fondness of all country lads for firearms practice, a relative of the family who had been a scout on the plains of the Far West and had won repute as a dead-center shot, paid a long visit to the Samuel farm. He drilled the boys in plain and fancy marksmanship. They had known only the one-barrel shotgun. This Wild Westerner introduced them to the rifle and the revolver. Under his tutelage the boys made rapid progress toward preparedness for their upcoming military life, not to mention their anti-social careers which followed.

Frank James enlisted under one of the lieutenants of Sterling Price, commander of the Missouri State Guards (of Southern persuasion). He fought in the fierce battle of Wilson Creek near Springfield, in southwest Missouri, on August 10, 1861. It was there the Federal commander, Gen. Nathaniel Lyon, of Connecticut origin, perished in a heroic effort to hold back the advancing hordes of General Price and Gen. Ben McCulloch (the latter being of the regular Confederate forces). With the exception of the first battle of Bull Run, three weeks earlier, Wilson Creek was the first important clash of arms in the Civil War.

Frank James paid a visit to the homefolks some months after Wilson Creek and was frank and fiery in advocacy of the Southern cause. He is said to have flourished a Colt's navy pistol somewhat threateningly by way of emphasizing his political leanings. Local Federal militia, of course, resented this, and the young soldier was arrested and locked in the little jail at Liberty, the Clay County seat. An oath of loyalty to the Union, signed

"Franklin James," apparently had no effect, for when Frank got out of jail he remained loyal to the Confederacy and proved it some time later by joining the growing squad of young daredevils led by William C. Quantrill, the renegade guerrilla chieftain, who had come from Ohio by way of Kansas.

Afterward, Jesse also was caught up into the guerrilla outfit, though not directly under Quantrill. The boy had remained at home during his brother's earlier wartime activities, having been too young then for soldiering. He was cultivating corn, trudging between the handles of an old-time bull-tongue plow one day in June, 1863, when the Hell's imps, which for years had been raging all around him, swooped down and with fingers not altogether phantasmal, clutched him, carried him aloft, shook him violently for a time, and then let him drop into the midst of the fiery furnace.

Jesse had not been burning with zeal for the cause which ultimately became lost. He did not intend to permit himself to be burned up in the hellfire of border hatred if he could help it. And he was able, as it turned out, to spit some fire himself.

That June day, a large squad of Federal militia visited the Samuel farm. Dr. Samuel, stepfather of the James boys, met the visitors and inquired as to their mission.

"You have been entirely too loud in your disloyal expressions," the leader informed him, "and so has your wife. Furthermore, you folks are friendly to that damn cutthroat Quantrill, and you harbor his men. We've come to teach you a lesson."

One of the regulators produced a stout cord, and the doctor's hands were bound behind his back. He was escorted to a tall tree with an overhanging limb. A rope was noosed about his neck, one end tossed over the limb and caught by several soldiers as it descended. They pulled hard, drawing the victim up until his feet were well off ground. The pulling end of the rope was then tied around the trunk of the tree; the doctor was left, presumably, to choke slowly to death.

Mrs. Samuel saved his life. She had followed the execution party, keeping considerably to the rear. As soon as the militiamen departed, she ran forward and cut her husband down. She was an excellent nurse; he, a skillful physician.

Though about half-dead from strangulation, Dr. Samuel recovered. His escape from death was due chiefly to the zeal of his tormentors, because of their haste to complete the rest of their job—they went to look for little Jesse. They found him in a distant cornfield, plowing as straight a row as any lad of fifteen could be expected to plow. He was a rather baby-faced boy, seeming younger even than his years. The lesson-teachers had another rope along, but, when they saw what a little fellow Jesse was, they hesitated.

"Don't let's hang him—this time," the leader counseled. "He's too young to go and fight like that tall, wild devil, Frank. But let's teach the cub a lesson, anyhow." The lesson comprised a whipping, along between the rows of corn. One of the teachers used the stout rope as a lash. Jesse released the plow handles and made toward home, the stern schoolmaster administering more of the lesson at every step. The militiamen made off, before the pupil got to the farmhouse to teach similar lessons to other Southern sympathizers.

When Jesse reached the house, running hard, his eyes were blinking more rapidly than ever. As a child, he had suffered from granulated eyelids. Throughout the rest of his life, he had the involuntary habit of frequent blinking. His eyes were large, of a light blue shade,* and tearful as well as blinking, when he reached the farmhouse. The boy was hurt both physically and spiritually. That ropelashing had been an insult as well as an

---

*This chronicler has no prejudicial attitude with regard to blue eyes; in fact, he is measurably fond of them. But it is a simple fact set down here that virtually all of the noted outlaws he has known in his long experience as a journalist have had blue eyes. The eyes of most of them were of a steel-blue tint. Frank James had such eyes; so also had Jim Cummins. The most spectacular bank robber that ever lived, the late Henry Starr of Oklahoma, who does not belong to the present narrative, sighted along the barrels of his six-shooters with eyes serenely blue.

injury. The proud old Kentucky-pioneer blood of the Jameses and the Coles was outraged. Jesse James was crying not only from physical pain, but from humiliation.

"What have they done to you?" demanded his mother, whose eyes were dry.

Jesse mumbled out what they had done to him. The back of his blue-check workshirt was damp with sweat—and with something else.

"Come here," commanded his mother. Jesse had been making for the water trough in the back yard.

"You come right here to me!"

Jesse obeyed his mother. She turned him around, grabbed a handful of the wet garment and drew the shirt up over his shoulders, exposing the boy's bare back. It was livid with long welts, from some of which blood trickled. Then, for the first time since the military visitation, Zerelda Samuel began to weep.

"Don't cry, Ma," the boy pleaded. "Don't you cry, now. I hate to see you cry—I just can't stand it, Ma. I'll go and join Quantrill and get even."

Members of Quantrill's command were in the neighborhood. After the resuscitated Dr. Samuel had attended to his welts and Mrs. Samuel had provided him with a clean shirt, Jesse went and found some of the infamous raiders and begged them to take him along as a member of the guerrilla force. They laughed at him. Quantrill couldn't use little blue-eyed babies, they said. Jesse returned home, disappointed and chagrined. Plowing corn had lost its interest for Jesse.

Some days later the regulators reappeared. This time, they were determined to kill both Dr. Samuel and Jesse James. They had heard that Jesse had failed to take his lesson seriously: he had been in communication with Quantrill's men, no doubt giving them valuable information—he had "informed" on the Federal militia.

Both the doctor and his stepson happened to be away from home. But the doctor's wife was there, and her daughter, little Susie James. Susie was twelve years old—goin' on thirteen. Mrs. Samuel and Susie were arrested—military arrest.

They were placed in jail at St. Joseph, Missouri, as persons disloyal to the Union. Their incarceration lasted for several weeks. There were also the two little Samuels, quite too young to hurt the Union or to help the Confederacy, whom the Federal authorities permitted Mrs. Samuel to take along to jail, Sallie Samuel, just past three years, and Johnnie, about fourteen months.*

When Mrs. Samuel was liberated and returned home, Jesse's back was no longer black and blue, but his eyes were as blue as ever, and they blinked fast and furiously when he greeted his mother.

"Ma, it's a damned outrage; that's what it is!" blubbered Jesse.

"Hush, son! You haven't been brought up to swear."

"Huh!" ejaculated Jesse, and a moment later his chubby round face was a flower garden of smiles. As boy and man, he could smile at slightest provocation. He could smile, and he did, in a certain manner, when putting a bullet through the head or heart of soldier or citizen. There were times when Jesse James had what some have been pleased to term a "disarming" smile.

---

*Incidentally, the next-born of the Samuel family was named in honor of Mr. W. C. Quantrill, though his name was misspelled, as usual, in the christening: Fannie Quantrill Samuel. The guerrilla chieftain's name was actually "Charles W. Quantrell." It is to be assumed that Fannie's name, had she been born a boy, would have been Charles Q. Samuel. Let us also pause to record the birth of the last-born of the Samuel children, Archie Payton Samuel, on July 22, 1866. Archie, at the age of eight and a half years, is a tragic little figure in a later chapter of this narrative.

2

Jim Cummins lived on a farm that had been his birthplace, a few miles from the Samuel homestead. Jim was about eight months older than Jesse James. The boys had played together from time to time. Jim was a thin stripling and Jesse, himself, a slight lad when the pair, with two other boys of the neighborhood, left home together and joined a guerrilla force affiliated with the groups under George Todd and Bill Anderson. The squad the four boys joined was under the immediate command of one Fletcher Taylor, who made a remarkable record as a fighter. As "Fletch" Taylor, his name is written redly in the annals of the Quantrillians, and, as Charles F. Taylor, after the war, he made a fortune in the lead and zinc mines at Joplin, Missouri.

Jesse and Jim presently got under the wing of Bloody Bill Anderson, who said of Jesse at sixteen, "For a beardless boy, he is the best fighter in the command." George Shepherd, another of Quantrill's and Anderson's most expert shooters and looters, and a future member of the James-Younger outlaw band, also extended a fatherly arm around Jesse toward the end of the war.

Instead of going to Kentucky, as Frank James did, on Quantrill's foolish and fatal expedition at the end of 1864, Jesse went to Texas with George Shepherd and some other veteran guerrillas. Although the boy had suffered ghastly wounds in battle, he was to suffer another, no less ghastly, when he returned to Missouri to surrender.

Post-bellum banditry in Missouri began with a St. Valentine's Day surprise party. The gentle saint of love and romance, however, had nothing to do with it, either in inspiration or in execution. The "function" was altogether the creation of a combination of demon-gods, who operated in the war-disordered brains of a dozen young daredevils who had ridden and robbed and slaughtered with Quantrill, Anderson, and Todd. All of these men, according to popular belief and the law of probabilities, were ex-guerrillas, less than a year out of the crimson course of the border Civil War.

Liberty, the county seat of the Jameses' native Clay county, was the town selected for the first manifestation of peacetime violence. Weary of the war which had raged around the place for a decade, irregular and regular, little Liberty was glad to be at peace again. Many of the undesirable citizens of Clay and the adjacent counties had departed, never to return. Hundreds of them, along with perhaps just as many desirable citizens, had fallen in the fray. Some had suffered strangulation at the noose-ends of ropes, dangling from convenient trees.

Many others, kit and boodle, had drawn stakes and decamped. For these, the changed conditions in Clay and Ray and Platte and Jackson Counties had become uncomfortable, not to say menacing. Men who had fought for the Union had "come in" and settled down again. Enemies of years past had become friends—with reservations. Everybody was heartily glad that the war was over—with exceptions.

The exceptions were some of the young fellows who didn't seem to know the war was over. Hard riding and straight shooting had become their habitual exercise. On scores of raids they had ridden, stirruped and spurred and six-shootered, hooting, shooting, looting. They had taken, by violence, what they needed, or what they wanted. Horses for fresh mounts, store merchandise, household goods—any sort of plunder which they fancied, had been theirs without the asking. Only the bullet had spoken.

In 1866 St. Valentine's day dawned bright and cold. The sun shed slanting rays upon the roof of the county courthouse, which, quite unknown to the sheriff and his deputies who were a bit late that morning in getting to their offices, was to become, that very day and for more than sixteen years afterward, the center of the world's most amazing manhunt.

Business places fronting on the courthouse square were opening. The hour was eight o'clock. Girls of romantic inclination, on their way to school, were stopping by the post office to inquire for mail, hoping that the youths they fancied had sent them valentines, and fearing that they had not. A few grinning lads who had mailed "comics" to the girls were lounging about in the hope of watching their victims open the merry missives. It was "business as usual" in Liberty, though early in the day for most of the population to be out.

On the hill beyond the public square sat William Jewell College, a Baptist institution then in its early years. Students who lived or boarded in the town were beginning to gather around the college. One of these was "Jolly" Wymore, son of a well-to-do citizen. His first name was George, but his disposition was such that nearly everybody called him Jolly. He was a bright lad of nineteen, who had perhaps more friends than any other student at William Jewell. Jolly was the life of many a party, where the young people gathered to play such games as kiss-your-partner.

Liberty being mostly Baptist, Methodist, and Presbyterian, dancing was taboo. Jolly Wymore, ambitious to earn his diploma and make his way in the world, accepted his share of the kisses without letting the pleasant pastime interfere seriously with his studies.

Little Jimmy Sandusky, several years younger than Jolly, was another college student on his way to school, books and slate under arm, his neck muffled with one of those oldtime "nubies" that kept small boys from getting the larynx chilled. The nubia conserved and deepened the effect of the vocal cords, so that Jimmy and his playmates could yell almost like grown men, almost—yet not quite so loudly and so fiercely!

Jolly Wymore and Jimmy Sandusky were to hear, that crisp February morning, the wild Rebel yell of the earlier Sixties, made wilder far than when it "rang through Shiloh's woods and Chickamauga's solitudes." It was the border guerrilla's modification of the more modest and less frightening Rebel yell of the true "fierce South cheering on her sons." It was, to describe the indescribable, the howl of the hyena, the yelp of the jackal, the yip-yip-yaw-aw-aw of a regular human devil riding, hell-bent for blood and booty. It was the baleful bleat of the men who had followed Blood-luster Quantrill and Bloody Bill Anderson into battle and ridden out with smoking pistols. It was the most terrifying sound that any human being ever heard.

At the northwest corner of the Liberty square, on that long-gone day, stood the substantial brick building in which the Clay County Savings Association did its banking business. Although the bank was as solid as the building, shortly after that day, it would liquidate its business and cease to be. The shock the bank was to receive that morning more than a century ago would wreck it as a financial institution. It was the shock of an onset of a round dozen of he-devil youths lately released from the restraints of organized war. They were graduates of guerrilla-ism, bearing diplomas that made them bachelors of free-bootery. Some of the dozen were, in time, to acquire their master's degree.

Fortunately, not only the bank building itself is a standing relic of the first bank raid, robbery and murder committed by these graduates, but there was also a living eyewitness to that historic crime. Little James Sandusky, later Judge James Sandusky, saw it and heard it. The judge supplied this writer with this brief page out of his past:

> I saw that bank robbery at Liberty, in February, 1866. I was only a boy. I was on my way to college, and when I was about half a block away, I saw several men sitting on their horses in the middle of the street in front of the bank. One of them fired and killed a student, George Wymore, about nineteen years old, standing on the corner of the street across from the bank. In a short time, other men came out of the bank, mounted their horses, and rode east on Franklin Street, about three blocks, then turned north and left town. They took the road leading from Liberty to what is now Excelsior Springs, and they crossed the Missouri river that night at some point in Ray County.
>
> As they were leaving town, a few citizens ran into the street firing at them, and they returned the fire. The sheriff and a posse pursued them, but not one was ever captured. There were no other injuries.

About sixty thousand dollars was taken, and lost—forty-five thousand in United States bonds, and the balance, in gold and currency. That night there was a blinding snowstorm, and it was intensely cold. The snowstorm helped the robbers make a clean getaway.

More than eight months passed before another bank was robbed by the mysterious Missourians. The snow had melted from the grave of Jolly Wymore; spring and summer had brought their gifts of grass and flowers, autumn's early frosts had begun, and hectic leaves began to drift upon the mound. Gone, but assuredly not forgotten, were the bank raiders. They had ridden straight back into the Nowhere whence they came.

Apparently, so far as Liberty was concerned, the incident was closed. But, late in October of that year—1866—five horsemen entered the battle-scarred town of Lexington and drew rein over the banking house of Alexander Mitchell and Company. It was noon. Business had yielded to the invitation of the dinner bell. The bank was deserted. Cashier J. L. Thomas, having nothing else to do, stood in the doorway looking idly across the street, chewing a quill toothpick. Disinterestedly, the cashier watched five men dismount and hitch their horses in an adjacent alley. He observed that all the horses were fine lookers. Two of the men walked slowly toward the bank. The cashier went back behind his counter: evidently a bit of banking business was in the offing.

The two strangers advanced to the cashier's window. One drew forth a fifty-dollar bond which might or might not have been one of those missing from Liberty. In those days, U.S. Bonds of fifty and one hundred dollars were used, for convenience, like ordinary currency.

"Can you change this for me, if you please, sir?" requested the holder.

"I reckon I can," the cashier replied, pleasantly. He opened the cash drawer and was figuring some currency when he glanced up and saw four big revolvers pointing directly at his head. Two more men had appeared in the doorway with Colt's navies—not concealed.

Cashier Thomas recalled the Liberty affair and accepted the situation with as much calmness as he could muster.

"Now give me all the money you have in the bank," suavely demanded the man who had asked for the change. "Do it quietly and quickly and you won't be hurt; but if you don't, you'll get your head blown off."

Thomas complied, quickly and quietly.

"All right; thanks," said the polite robber, tossing the loot into a wheat sack held open by the man standing at his side. "Now don't you give an alarm, for if you do you'll be too dead to know it."

The two men backed to the door, keeping the cashier covered with their weapons. The two at the door backed away, pocketing their pistols. The four of them walked at normal gait into the alley, where the fifth had remained looking after the horses. They all unhitched, turned into the street, and rode out of town without any further ado.

They may have been ex-guerrillas—most probably they were—though none of them uttered the terrifying yell. It was a quick and quiet affair throughout.

Cashier Thomas waited until the clatter of the hoofs had died almost to silence before he walked out and informed the neighboring merchants that these five horsemen had robbed the bank of all the cash on hand—two thousand dollars.

It was an hour or so, before a dozen Lexington men found mounts and set out in the direction taken by the robbers. The posse spent a couple of days in riding about the country, making various inquiries, striking a possible trail here and there. Nothing come of the pursuit, save weariness and vexation.

A public meeting was held in Lexington, the idea being that something should be done about the matter. Country banks should be safeguarded, if possible, against such incursions. There was that Liberty affair, the bank there lost sixty thousand dollars, and a fine young man had been murdered. These two James boys of Clay County, wild young fellows by reputation, had been suspected at Liberty: well, probably they and their gang had robbed the Lexington bank. Beyond that, nobody had a theory. After a few weeks the mild excitement subsided, though the personnel of small-town banks through that general section of Missouri felt uneasy.

Lexington is on the southern bank of the Missouri River, a day's easy horseback ride east of Liberty and southeast of the James boys' home. Savannah, seat of Andrew County, where the daylight bank robbers made their third appearance, is a couple of days' journey by dirt road to the northwest part of the Samuel farm. Four months intervened between the Lexington and Savannah affairs.

The private bank of Judge McLain was the financial stronghold of Savannah. On the second of March, 1867, five horsemen rode leisurely into the little town. The hour was twelve o'clock, almost the same, to the minute, as the time of the Lexington robbery. As at Lexington, most of the townspeople were indoors at dinner.

Judge McLain and his son were in the bank alone, until four of the five strangers entered. The fifth was left to guard the horses hitched nearby. Apparently, Banker McLain had the Lexington affair in mind. He figured that it must be the same gang on a similar errand.

The banker was a man of nerve. Without waiting for his visitors to make an initial demonstration, he slammed his safe door shut, snatched his pistol from its shelf under the cash counter, and began firing at the quartet as rapidly as he could cock his weapon and pull the trigger.

A brave man—but a bad marksman!

The four men drew their weapons at the moment Judge McLain drew his. All returned his fire. The wonder is that he was not shot to shreds in that close battle, but only one bullet hit him. A ball from a Colt's navy revolver penetrated his breast, and he fell heavily to the floor. Meantime, McLain's son had rushed out into the street, bullets whizzing about his ears, and cried the alarm.

Unharmed, the thwarted robbers ran out to their horses and sped away with the fifth rider. They got not a penny of the McLain bank money. Savannah citizens were somewhat quicker than the Lexingtonians had been; mounts were found almost immediately, and the fugitives were pursued by a few men. By mid-afternoon, nearly all the horses in town, and a number from outlying farms, had been mounted by enraged citizens and were galloping out one road or another. Groups were absent on the trail for several days, but nobody was caught.

"The James gang again!" cried many more than one. "Looks just like one of their jobs, from all a fellow hears."

A couple of men, Samuel Pope and William McDaniels (the latter was known as "Bud"), were arrested some time later on suspicion. They had alibis, though, and went free. Bud McDaniels, a Kansas City man, if he was not a member of the James-Younger gang then, became one later; and he will reappear later in this narrative.

William Chiles, James White, and J. F. Edmunson, former guerrillas, also were suspected of complicity in the Savannah failure, but none was apprehended. Judge McLain recovered from his wound and was a local hero for years.

3

Violent events now were coming fast. Less than three months after Savannah, came Richmond, that pleasant little city, the seat of Ray County, immediately east of Clay. It is less than a dozen miles northwest of Lexington. Ray County was to become, in time, an important part of the Jesse James country, with a certain farmhouse near Richmond as an intimate center of operations more tragic than comic, though they were both. From that lowly homestead visited time and again by Frank and Jesse James, Jim Cummins, and other members of the outlaw fraternity, was to go forth, middle-aged, the career of the king of the bandits. And in that same house, not long before the end of Jesse James, one member of his band was to meet violent death at the hands of another member.

In the matter of fatalities resulting from the Richmond bank robbery of May 23, 1867, this was the bloodiest of all the raids allegedly ridden upon by the James-Younger combine. The deaths of at least eight persons may be traced thereto.

If the Lexington five and the Savannah five were one and the same quintet, as appearances suggested, then it was not unlikely that the Liberty and Richmond dozens were the same men, with a few more added to the group. Some citizens averred that they counted fourteen men in the gang of robbers and murderers who invaded Richmond. This outfit, mounted on fast horses and emitting the unmistakable Rebel guerrilla yell, dashed into town firing right and left. Citizens ducked and darted hither and yon. Six of the mounted miscreants halted at the Hughes and Mason Bank, the doors of which had been closed and locked when the yelping devils were heard from afar.

With the other members of the gang sitting on their horses shooting and hooting, the six broke into the bank and found about four thousand dollars, which they crammed into the customary sack. Out again, they rejoined their accomplices, who, by now, were having much less fun than they had at first. Mayor Shaw of Richmond was the chief official hero of the tragic day. Somewhere he had found a hefty six-shooter, and he dashed across the street to a point where other citizens who showed some fight were gathering. Apparently, it was the mayor's purpose to take lead of this impromptu posse, but before he reached the spot, he was observed by three of the yelling riders, who charged down upon him. The mayor fired briskly at the trio, but they were too many for him. He went down—the autopsy later showing four bullets in his body.

In the county jail, adjoining the courthouse and not far from the bank, were several prisoners who, it was alleged afterward by friends of the suspected ex-guerrillas, were held there because they had continued to express secessionist sentiments. The raiders made a bold attempt to break open the jail and liberate these men. B. G. Griffin, the jailer, and his son, a courageous lad of fifteen, sought to withstand the assault. The boy got a big revolver and took up a post behind a tree, from which inadequate shelter he was firing upon the murderous gang when they shot him dead. Jailer Griffin saw his son fall; he rushed forward and stood over the boy's body, shooting at the murderers. It took seven bullets to strike him down. Several of his wounds were in vital parts, and the father fell dead across his dead son.

With their sack of loot, the fourteen bandits finally galloped out of Richmond, evidently having suffered no injury from the citizens' bullets. This outrage aroused the whole county and several counties adjacent, not omitting Clay and Jackson. The whole of the Jesse James country stood up in anger. Men of means subscribed to a fund for running down robbers and murderers. Warrants were issued for eight men who were alleged to have been recognized as members of the gang. These were James White, John White, Payne Jones, Richard Burns, Isaac Flannery, Andrew McGuire, Thomas Little, and Allen H. Parmer. Most of them had served under either Quantrill, Bill Anderson, or George Todd.

Allen Parmer, who, three years later, was to become brother-in-law to the Jameses by marrying Miss Susan L. James, had been one of Quantrill's most deadly marksmen; he had made a gory record at the Lawrence Massacre.

As to the Richmond affair, Parmer had a perfect alibi, it having been proven that he was working at an honest job, in Kansas City, when the raid took place.

Three days after the Richmond tragedy, and on the day of the funerals of the three local victims, a posse of about twenty men from Kansas City learned that Payne Jones was in a certain house near Independence. The posse went out after him. It was a rainy night, of pitchy darkness. A little girl, named Noland, was taken along as guide. Members of the posse surrounded the house as quietly as possible, but Jones discovered their presence. He flung open a door and bolted out, a double-barrel shotgun in his hands and two Colt's six-shooters in his belt.

The desperado discharged both barrels of his gun before the startled posse could appreciate the situation. B. H. Wilson, a young member of the posse, was killed, and the Noland girl wounded so seriously, that she died in a short time. Jones threw down his shotgun, drew his pistols, and made for the woods. He was pursued for some miles. Many shots were fired in the darkness, by both Jones* and his pursuers, but none found a living target.

The Missouri counties of Clay and Jackson had become decidedly inhospitable territory for the Jameses and the Youngers. There were only a few homes where never a door was closed against them in all the years of their outlawry. Save those, the young men kept themselves invisible to the public eye in their own country for many months following the Richmond tragedy. Though not under indictment, they were under suspicion, and discreet enough to veil themselves effectually from the view

---

*Some years later, Payne Jones was murdered by a former guerrilla comrade who had borne him a grudge, and the night following the Payne Jones tragedy, a posse of Richmond men ran down Richard Burns. Convinced of his guilt, they took him to a lonely spot far off in the woods. Burns begged for time to pray, which was denied him. He was hanged from a tree without trial. His bones were found some time later—picked clean by crows and buzzards.

of officers of the law and private detectives. The Pinkertons, who in years to come were to have tragic relations with both the Youngers and the Jameses, already were beginning to scent the trails of the outlaw suspects.

Far ahead upon those trails, the lifeblood of three or more Pinkerton operatives was to soak into the soil of Missouri and cry out for vengeance; and vengeance, responding, was to operate in two directions. For nearly a year, all was quiet along the Missouri, but on the twentieth of March, 1868, Missouri bandit bullets were heard in Kentucky. That day the first of the bank robberies by the ex-guerrillas was committed beyond the borders of Missouri, in the town of Russellville.

James Younger and Frank James, who had invaded Kentucky with Quantrill early in 1865 and participated in a series of engagements, already had bad names in that state because of those activities. But Jesse James and Coleman Younger were but vague names to Kentuckians—until the Russellville raid.

This quiet little Logan County town of about three thousand people had no suspicion that any of the rough-riding Missourians were even in the vicinity, until six men rode in, wounded two citizens, and rode out with about fourteen thousand dollars from the safe of the local bank.

4

The James boys' trip to California was in the hope, on the part of their friends and themselves, that some time spent far from the scenes of their youthful activities might improve their chances for settling down and living like other folks.

"Stay away a while, boys, and it will all blow over," was the advice they acted upon. There is no reason to doubt that they had more than enough of the violent life, and that the simple life appealed strongly to both of them, perhaps more strongly to Frank than to Jesse.

But it didn't "blow over." When they returned to Clay County and made that discovery, they began to feel that they were in for it as a permanent proposition, and they began to seek out what virtue might be found in violence. It was then, and not till then, that the Jameses become desperate outlaws in full fact. Despairing of a peaceful future, desperation became their portion. They had gotten started wrong, and they couldn't stop without bending their necks for the noose.

When in California the boys went to a tintype "artist" and, standing together, had a likeness of themselves made, which they sent to their mother. Mrs. Samuel had the picture set in a locket which she wore on her bosom beneath her dress all the rest of her life.

If the Pinkerton detectives had killed Mrs. Samuel when they tossed a bomb into her house in January, 1875, instead of merely blowing off her right forearm, they might have found, on her bosom, a specific aid to identifying her outlaw sons. One of the principal reasons why the Jameses were never arrested lay in the fact that the sleuths had no pictures by which to identify them. That the boys, knowing that they would be hanged if apprehended, were determined never to be taken alive, was only ancillary.

Not often did Jesse James leave a clue to his identity when he galloped away from a crime of violence. On one most memorable occasion, however, he did so, only because on this occasion he left the horse he had ridden in from the awesome Nowhere.

Though Jesse had an alibi ready-made, and his friends had another man to thrust into his place at this robbery, the unspoken testimony of his own high-stepping steed remained sufficient proof to the people of Daviess County, Missouri, that he helped rob the Daviess County Savings Bank at Gallatin, and that it must have been Jesse who shot down the cashier, Capt. John W. Sheets.

This double crime took place on December 7, 1869, more than twenty months after the Russellville raid. It signified, after a long absence, the definite reentry of the James-Younger combination into their old home state.

In the intervening period, the Missouri outlaws had been quiet enough to satisfy the most exacting advocate of law and order.

The Gallatin affair was accomplished by a force much smaller than usually went on a raid against a bank. The average number of men staging a raid was about six. At Gallatin, only three men were in the party. There seems to be less ground for believing that Younger was present, than for the conviction that both the Jameses were on hand. Nobody was recognized or identified, or captured, and nobody confessed. One must rely solely upon circumstantial evidence to fix the responsibility for that un-punished crime, and the circumstance of the horse is difficult to explain away.

The robbery and murder may be described briefly: without any demonstration suggesting former guerrillaism, the three men rode into Gallatin. They were quiet and orderly as they approached the bank. Two of them dismounted and entered; the third remained with the horses, his business being also to serve as lookout.

Captain Sheets, who had been a Federal officer during the war, and a young man named McDowell, who was making a deposit, were the only persons present until the bandits entered.

One robber laid a hundred-dollar bill on the cashier's counter and requested that it be changed into smaller bills. Captain

Sheets picked up the bill and was counting out the change, when the other outlaw thrust a Colt's navy toward him and demanded that he surrender the keys to the inner doors of the safe. (The outer door was already open.)

The man who had requested the changing of the bill now presented a weapon and held Captain Sheets captive while his accomplice went in back of the counter and took about seven hundred dollars from the safe and till.

The two robbers whispered together for a moment, both intently studying the face of the cashier. An instant later, the one who had kept Sheets covered with his revolver pulled the trigger. The cashier fell dead.

Two or three citizens had already tried to enter the bank on business. Threatening death, the man on guard outside had driven them off. They had given the alarm, and several men had snatched up such firearms as were close at hand and were gathering near the bank. The lookout called to his accomplices to hurry out.

Already they were at the door. They rushed for their horses, the other man having mounted. The man carrying the bank money got into his saddle, and he and the lookout were off, but the fellow who had shot Sheets had poor luck. Bullets were whistling. Shouts were heard above the shots. The spirited animal which the third outlaw was trying to mount plunged and snorted. His rider had one foot in the stirrup when the horse dashed away, dragging the man some yards. Struggling, the fellow succeeded in releasing himself, and his horse trotted away to a livery stable, probably preferring the company of his own kind.

One of the mounted robbers rode back, the fallen one was helped up behind him, and the double-laden horse carried his burden out of town, pistols cracking both from and toward the escaping outlaws. Within a few minutes, several live-wire Gallatin men got horses and began pursuit. They felt reasonably confident of capturing the two men on one horse. But a mile or so southwest of the town, the fugitives met a farmer, Daniel Smoot, riding into Gallatin on a capable horse.

"Get down—and get away!" cried the robbers.

Smoot complied, seeing two large weapons pointing at him. He disappeared into a field. The man who had been riding behind mounted Smoot's horse. The three desperadoes thus easily outdistanced the pursuing parties. When near the small town of Kidder some miles from Gallatin, they impressed a Methodist preacher into service.

"You know the roads," he was told. "Pilot us around this town so we won't have to go through it."

The preacher did as he was told. Under the circumstances, he became as honest, though by no means as earnest, at land-piloting as he was at sky-piloting. Just before the bandits advised him that he was free to proceed on his way in peace, the one who was riding the Smoot steed remarked:

"I'm Bill Anderson's brother. I've just killed S. P. Cox—if I'm not mistaken in the man I shot. Cox killed my brother, and now I've killed Cox for vengeance. Been after him for five years. Good-bye, parson."

Lieut. S. P. Cox of the Federal Army was the man whose bullet was supposed to have been the one that finished the career of Bloody Bill Anderson, who fell in a running fight with some soldiers in Ray County, Missouri, in the autumn of 1864. Jesse James, at that time, was a member of the guerilla force commanded by Anderson.

The sheriff of Daviess County took possession of the horse that had refused to carry his rider out of town. It was an excellent piece of horseflesh, a large and living clue to the identity of the man who had shot Captain Sheets. The problem was simple enough, provided that the man who rode the horse into Gallatin was the owner. The animal, of course, might have been stolen.

The public's nine days' wonder as to whose horse it was came to an end on December 16, when the *Kansas City Times* carried a news story conveying the information that the mount had been identified, beyond question, as the property of "a young man named James, whose mother and stepfather live about four miles from Centerville, Clay County, near the Cameron branch of the Hannibal and Saint Joe Railroad."

When two men from Gallatin arrived at Liberty with proof of the identity of Jesse James's horse that had broken loose and remained at the scene of the crime, local sentiment demanded prompt action against the owner of the mount. The owner's brother was also included in this demand, for officials of Clay County felt reasonably sure that Frank had been with Jesse at Gallatin.

Capt. John S. Thomason, formerly sheriff of the county, lived in Liberty. He had served in the regular Confederate Army and was a highly respected citizen. Both as sheriff and as army officer, he had given abundant proof of personal courage and solid common sense. He felt that, for the honor of Clay County, he should lead an expedition to the home of the Jameses and bring the boys back with him to Liberty, where they would have the opportunity to render an account of their deeds.

Captain Thomason owned a saddlehorse of which he was justifiably proud; it was a splendid steed that had carried him through many a battle. He saddled this animal, polished his army pistols, and, with his son Oscar and two or three other well-mounted and properly pistoled men, set forth on the road to the Samuel farm.

"We'll bring the boys in," said the captain as his party left the courthouse square.

"All right, captain; we'll do the rest," gaily promised a spokesman for the circuit court official staff.

The Jameses saw them coming. Frank and Jesse had already learned the value of vigilance. They advanced down the road to meet the enemy. They knew the Thomasons and were aware that the captain had been a gallant Confederate. There was brief parley, in voices loud enough to carry across a considerable distance.

"We want you boys to come to Liberty with us," announced Captain Thomason.

"We don't want to go to Liberty, and we don't intend to go," announced one of the Jameses.

"But you've got to come along," insisted the captain.

"Not until we get good and ready."

The next proceeding had to do with firearms practice, though the James boys apparently had no desire to kill any of the possemen. It seems they merely wished to shoo them away.

Both sides fired. Nobody was hit. But, when it became evident to Jesse James that the Liberty men meant stern business, he shot to kill—a horse. Taking good aim, he put a bullet through the head of Captain Thomason's veteran war-horse. The animal dropped dead, his rider sliding off without injury. By this time, the skirmish had taken both pursuers and pursued out of sight of the old homestead. The Jameses drew off, as did the deputies. Frank and Jesse disappeared from the neighborhood. Captain Thomason, after witnessing their discreet flight, walked up to the Samuel farmhouse and borrowed a horse from the stable.

"Your son Jesse has killed my horse," he told Mrs. Samuel.

"Well, captain," said the militant mother, "I reckon you're in great luck, at that, for Jesse must have killed your horse to keep from having to kill you."

"Maybe so—I don't know. But I'll see that he pays for my horse, some way," declared the indignant captain. "Those boys of yours, Mrs. Samuel, are getting entirely too wild."

"Why don't you people let my boys alone, Captain Thomason? If you did, they wouldn't be so wild."

Tradition states that there was much more give-and-take talk between the two, with Mrs. Samuel's lecturing Captain Thomason and the captain's lecturing her. The mother of the Jameses could hold her own in any duel of tongues, and, at last, the posse leader and his men rode away.

When Thomason returned to Liberty riding the borrowed horse there was much indignation. But, although the captain was humiliated, his skin was whole, as were the hides of Oscar Thomason and the others, which was an item not to be despised in the reckoning. In the years that followed, such a casualty as the killing of a horse seemed utterly insignificant in the catalogue of crimson deeds charged up against the James boys. Some of Captain Thomason's cronies teased him, from time to time, about the loss of his war-horse, but, as the years sped, and as bullets sped manward instead of beastward, the incident was almost forgotten by the disinterested citizens.

But Jesse James remembered it:

One day Oscar Thomason and another man were standing together on a street in a Texas town talking, when a young man passed them and turned around and came back. He smiled, reached out a hand, and called both men by name: "Hello, Plunk; hello, Oscar." He was Jesse James.

"Oscar," he said to young Thomason, "I've been wanting to see you for years."

Jesse still smiled, but Oscar was wondering, maybe a bit uncomfortably, just why Jesse had been so eager to see him.

"Well, Jess," said Oscar, clearing his throat, which seemed just slightly husky, "here I am; anything I can do for you?"

"Nothing at all, Oscar," replied Jesse; "but I reckon maybe I can do something for you. I figure you haven't forgotten that time you and your father and those other fellows from Liberty tried to take me and Frank, up at the old home in Clay?"

"I should say not, Jess," Oscar admitted, trying hard to return Jesse's amiable smile.

Plunk stood silent, wondering what the dickens Jesse James had up his sleeve, so to speak. He knew how quick on the trigger Jesse was, for he had seen the young guerrilla pop off Federal soldiers, several in a bunch, firing six-shooters with both hands. He quite knew, of course, that Jesse had a couple of Colt's navies concealed on his person, ready-to-hand. That fact was as certain as daylight.

"Well," said Jesse, pulling out—no, not one of his big guns—pulling out a big fat pocketbook, "I've always been sorry I found it necessary to shoot that fine horse of your father's. Captain Thomason was a brave Confederate soldier. I didn't want to shoot him, so I shot his horse instead. I had to do it, Oscar. I always intended to pay the captain for that horse, but never got a chance. You fellows both know why. Since he died, I've been hoping to run across you somewhere, so I could pay up. How much, about, was the horse worth?"

"Well, Jess, I reckon—well, my father wouldn't have taken any money for that favorite animal of his, but I remember hearing him say that he had been offered a hundred and twenty-five dollars."

Jesse peeled off some bills from a roll out of his pocketbook and handed the cash to Oscar.

"Here's settlement for that old account, Oscar," he said, with a laugh. "I'm glad to get it off my mind."

Young Thomason obligingly took the money. After Jesse had talked with Plunk and Oscar for a few minutes longer about old times up in Clay, and asked about certain friends and enemies, all the while keeping his eyes blinking in every direction, he smiled himself away.

So there's a true story about Jesse James that's never been published.

5

The story of another early attempt to catch Jesse James at his old home has been mishandled miserably by many long-distance biographers. The date was more than a year prior to the Thomason episode resulting in the loss of the horse. In fact, it happened only a short time after the Liberty bank robbery. Jesse, as we learned in the account of that affair, was confined to his bed much of the time around that date, still suffering from a wound in his right lung that a soldier in a Wisconsin regiment had inflicted when the young guerrilla was going into Lexington, Missouri, to surrender, at the close of the war. After the boy had lain in the woods for a day or so, he had been picked up and taken to a farmhouse, where he received surgical attention and nursing.

Maj. B. J. Rodgers, of the regular army stationed at Lexington, was in charge of the bureau receiving surrenders and passing out paroles. He learned that Jesse's mother and her smaller children had gone to Nulla, a small town in Nebraska, to escape prosecution by the Federal militia. Dr. Samuel, her husband, had accompanied his family and was practicing medicine in and around Nulla.

Major Rodgers provided the transportation to send Jesse out to the Nebraska town, on a stretcher, so that the boy might have the comfort of dying under his mother's care. But Jesse refused to die there.

"Take me back home, Ma," he pleaded. "I don't want to die up here in the North."

His mother took him back. The whole family returned home. For many months, Jesse lay in bed, slowly recovering.

Shortly after the Liberty bank raid, the local militia determined to go out to the farm, arrest Jesse James, and see either that he was punished for his activities in the war, or were killed if he resisted arrest. They preferred, most likely, the latter course.

Six members of the home guard visited the Samuel homestead about midnight, late, in the unusually cold February. Jesse was asleep. Dr. Samuel responded to a loud rap on the door, inquiring who was there and what was wanted. This woke Jesse, who peered through a window and saw six horses and one man. The other men were posted at different points near the house; two or three were on the front porch.

Jesse got up, drew on his clothes, buckled his cartridge belt around him, and, with one of his big Colt's navy pistols in each hand, stood ready for the emergency. He was weak, but not shaky.

"We want Jesse James," said the leader of the party. "Open this door!"

Dr. Samuel made a pretense of the lock's being out of order, thus giving Jesse a brief time in which to prepare himself.

The man outside pounded on the door panel.

"Open this door! We want Jesse James—"

"Here I am," said Jesse. "Come and get me." He fired a shot through the door. The militiaman turned and fell dead on the doorstep.

On hearing the shot, the other five rushed to the front of the house. Jesse threw the door partly open, and the light from the snow made the men outside easy targets for his unerring aim, while he was so hidden by the door and the darkness within, that the attacking party could not fire with the least accuracy.

In half the time it has taken the reader even to scan this report, three of the six men were lying dead in the snow, two others were desperately wounded, and one had fled in mortal terror. Suffering, as he was, from a very high fever, Jesse lost no time in mounting his horse, and, with a hurried good-bye, he again rode into the wilderness, leaving his mother and her family with the dead and wounded.

It was a ghastly scene there upon the white-shrouded ground, one man dead on the doorstep, two others stiff and frozen in their own blood which crimsoned the yard, while the groans from the wounded made the place more hideous.

Jesse took refuge with relatives in Kentucky. The Jameses had many family connections in Logan and Nelson Counties, and those two sections of Kentucky became far-outlying provinces of the Jesse James country for many years to come.

6

The Jameses lasted through the decade; the Youngers dropped out about midway. But it was Minnesota, not Missouri, that saw the demise of the Youngers as a tribe, except for one of the four brothers, John, a minor figure in outlawry, and even John Younger was attended to, not by a state law-officer, but by a Pinkerton detective. Incidentally, John took the detective along with him into the Unknown Beyond, and Jim Younger sent another Pinkerton to swift doom at the same time.

Missouri had become known as "the Robber State," that being the descriptive title which her sister commonwealths were applying to her with no apologies. It was averred by reputable citizens that the values of Missouri real estate had depreciated quite seriously because of the outlaws' energetic pursuit of the business of robbing banks and railway trains. It is not to be questioned that many prospective settlers were shunted into other Mid-West states because they looked upon poor old Missouri, justifiably, as the robber state. Such was the terror created by thunder-bloody literature concerning the James and Younger outfit, that many timid tourists, undeniably, detoured before they reached the Missouri line and proceeded through adjacent states.

However, the Serious Seventies saw the Missouri bandits operating in several states other than their own, without making over those alien communities into areas of dread and depreciation. Happily, the year 1870 was a blank in the program of the bandits. Their first reappearance after the tragedy at Gallatin was on June 3, 1871, and, at that time, they went into the North a short distance.

In that interval, they had been rusticating in Kentucky, Texas, the Indian Territory, and possibly elsewhere; now and then, no doubt, in their own counties, Jackson and Clay, where they

43

kept so quiet that their presence was known only to their friends or possibly some enemies to whom discretion counseled silence.

The capital of Wayne County, Iowa, which bears the classic-sounding name of Corydon, is but a few miles above the Missouri border. Situated in the midst of a rich agricultural region, in the heart of the hog and corn belt, it seems to have been assumed by the outlaws that the bank at Corydon should supply packings worth their while.

Accordingly, on that rare June day, in 1871, they rode out of Missouri into Iowa—and out of Iowa into Missouri. Say what you may, those fellows loved poor old Missouri! They were always coming back.

Just who robbed the Ocobock Brothers Bank at Corydon, no man knows to this day. But certain signs indicated that it was the familiar Missouri gang. The bandits selected that particular day, no doubt, because an outdoor political meeting was to be in progress. There was public speaking in the courthouse square, and the bank robbery would be easy. So it turned out.

When the seven men rode into the town, nobody paid them any attention—just another group of young farmhands dressed in their Sunday clothes, coming in to hear the speeches. In those days, a political meeting in the Middle West possessed a pulling power far beyond the present strength of a similar gathering. Spellbinders awed the open-mouthed multitudes, and an army could have surrounded a town when some forensic celebrity was uttering wisdom or worse.

Three of the horsemen entered the bank and found the cashier all alone. Each man poked a pistol at the head of the cashier, who gave up the keys to the safe quickly.

The robbers took forty thousand dollars. Before leaving the bank, they bound the cashier, hand and foot, and gagged him.

This act was unlike any the Missouri outlaws had performed before or afterward; probably it arose from their desire to attend the political meeting. Those young men could talk politics with fluency, and they were Democrats in the midst of a Black

Republican stronghold, which, for the nonce, was listening to a Missouri Democrat of the rock-ribbed variety.

The orator of the day was the Honorable H. Clay Dean, a celebrated, brilliant, and eccentric politician and lawyer from Northern Missouri. The bandits rode from the bank to the public square, one of them holding the loot-sack between his saddle-horn and his belly. It looked, of course, just like an innocent purchase of some Corydon merchandising commodity and not at all like forty thousand dollars.

The eloquent namesake of Henry Clay was in the midst of a fiery oration on the evils of Black Republicanism. One of the bank robbers, sitting on his horse at the outskirts of the crowd—popularly supposed to be Jesse James (and it was just like Jesse to do it)—interrupted the speaker:

"Mr. Dean, I rise to a point of order, sir."

"What is it, friend and fellow-citizen?" inquired the orator. "If it is anything of paramount importance, I yield to the gentleman on horseback."

All Iowan eyes turned toward the mounted man, whose companions sat on their steeds close by.

"Well, sir," said Jesse James, "I reckon it's important enough. The fact is, Mr. Dean, some fellows have been over to the bank and tied up the cashier, and if you-all ain't too busy, you might ride over and untie him. I've got to be going."

Then the robbers rode away. Suspecting his interrupter merely of trying to annoy him, and not knowing that Jesse was a good Democrat, the Honorable Mr. Dean reknit the raveled threads of his speech. It was some minutes before the outlaw's hint was acted upon. By that time the indubitably bold raiders were well out of town. A posse followed, an hour later, after an argument as to which road the seven strangers had taken. The trail led into Clay and Jackson Counties—and Nowhere.

About two months after the Corydon robbery Clell Miller of Clay County, a former guerrilla and a recent recruit to the James-Younger band—in which company he remained until his violent death farther north—was arrested near his home by detectives from Kansas City. He was taken to Iowa after extradition proceedings, underwent a four-day trial at Corydon late in the next year, and was acquitted. The evidence was insufficient to identify him as one of the robbers.

Jameses and Youngers presented alibis, naming many persons in their home counties who, they averred, could testify to their presence in Missouri at the time the Iowa bank was robbed.

There was no jesting in connection with the next robbery supposed to have been committed by the James gang; Jesse James was one of the suspects. Five men robbed the Deposit Bank at Columbia, Adair County, Kentucky, on April 29, 1872. They entered the town on horseback by different roads, the group coming together in the public square at about half-past two o'clock in the afternoon. Three men went into the bank, the other two staying outside, firing revolvers for intimidation purposes.

Cashier R. A. C. Martin and two other men were in the bank. Martin refused to open the safe and was shot to death. The robbers got only the money in the cash drawer, about two hundred dollars. The whole party rode away without further incident.

The next raid by the Jameses was about 4 P.M., September, 23, 1872, in the Kansas City Fair Grounds. It was "Big Thursday," and about thirty thousand people had paid gate fees. Just as the man carrying the tin cashbox containing nearly ten thousand dollars stepped outside the main gate, three horsemen dashed up. People leaped aside to keep from being run over. One man dismounted, grabbed the money box, and handed it to one of the men still on horseback. Then he remounted, and the trio rode away, firing many shots into the air.

Sainte Genevieve Savings Association Bank ordinarily carried quite a bit of cash on hand. It has been averred that a hundred thousand dollars was not an unusual total for them to have on hand for any bandit outfit that might covet the currency. But, being so far from the Jesse James country, quaint little old Sainte Genevieve felt secure against bank looters.

The outlaws are believed to have ridden horseback all the way to Sainte Genevieve, by a roundabout route covering perhaps four hundred miles. First they rode southward, making a stop with friends at a rural place in the hill country south of Springfield, Missouri, "Queen City of the Ozarks." Then they turned eastward, riding through the heart of the rugged Ozark ridges to Bismarck, a town on the Iron Mountain Railroad, about seventy-five miles south of Saint Louis. There they spent a day resting up, man and horse. Resuming their long journey, they rode through Saint François and Sainte Genevieve Counties to the town of the latter name, arriving on the morning of May 21, 1873. Before they got to Sainte Genevieve the group split, two men riding in from the north, and three from the south.

O. D. Harris, cashier, and Firman A. Rozier, Jr., whose father was president of the Savings Association, were on duty. No customers were present. Three bandits went into the bank. All of them pointed pistols at Harris.

Young Rozier was ignored; he ran out into the street, yelling that the bank was in the hands of robbers and murderers. He was rather rash, at that, for the two robbers outside fired three bullets at him, one of which passed through the cloth of his coat.

"Open the safe door!" was the succinct command heard by Cashier Harris.

"I'm in your power, gentlemen," said the obliging cashier.

It so happened that the bank was far along in process of liquidation, a fact which the robbers' advance agent had failed to learn. Most of the cash on deposit had been sent to the Merchants Bank in Saint Louis. Instead of the expected hundred thousand, the raiders got only about four thousand, and much of that was in silver coin. The wheat sack was so heavy that it dragged the ground as they emerged from the bank with Harris walking in advance, pistol-persuaded. They permitted him to go about his business when all were mounted and ready to depart.

Not far out of town the horse of the bandit bearing the silver stumbled, and the bandit dropped the sack. The whole party halted while he got off his horse to pick up the treasure.

When he tried to remount, the unwieldy loot bag struck against the animal's flank; the coins made a clinky sound; and the beast broke loose and bounded back toward Sainte Genevieve.

A pretty pickle for hardworking coin-collectors! At this immediate moment a German-American farmer came riding a horse toward town.

"Here, you—ride hard after that loose horse and catch him—bring him back here—quick!"

"Und vot do I get?"

"You get the horse, damn your Dutch hide! If you don't, you get a bullet right out of this Colt!"

The German looked at the muzzle of the six-shooter and rode hard after the loose horse. Some distance up the road he caught the animal. When he led it back and delivered it to the unmounted man, who had in the meantime turned over the sack of silver to a companion, he addressed the bandits again:

"Yah, I catch der horse, now. Vot do I get for dot?"

"You get avay mit your life, you tamned Tutchman! Vot else you egspeck, hey, alretty yet?"

Everybody laughed, excepting the "Dutchman," and once more the robbers rode away into their Nowhere.

7

Jesse James has been credited or discredited with having invented the art, science, or industry of train robbing. Well, perhaps Jesse James did invent train robbing. If not he, then some member of his gang must have been the inventor. Frank James and Jim Younger went westward about the time the Sainte Genevieve bank raiders started southeastward. They were under instructions to ascertain just when there was to be a big gold shipment from the West to the East.

There was to be such a shipment, by way of the Chicago, Rock Island, and Pacific Railway, about the third week in July of that year. The gold would be whizzing through the little town of Adair, July 21, 1873.

The seven robbers mounted their horses and rode to a point a few miles west of Adair, where a sharp curve presented excellent opportunity for wrecking a train. Hitching their horses in the woods, they unspiked a rail from the track. They left the loosened rail in place but tied a long rope around it. The end of the rope was held by a couple of the bandits who lay concealed in shrubbery and grass some yards from the track.

At 8:30 P.M., on time, Engineer John Rafferty, one of the Rock Island's most faithful men, drove his train around the curve, "hand on the throttle, eye on the track." John Rafferty was obeying regulations. His quick eye saw a rail, unaccountably yet nonetheless actually, move suddenly to the outside of the track, as if somebody had given it a quick jerk. Rafferty reversed, but the distance was fatally short. The huge locomotive plunged off the track and turned over on its side, crushing the engineer to death. The fireman was bruised but not injured seriously.

The train conductor assumed that the engine had left the rails at the curve because of some ordinary wrecking accident, but his assumption was dissipated when seven hooting, shooting desperadoes arose from the brush, some on one side, some on the other, and rushed to board the train. Even then, the conductor could not comprehend the situation. Train robbing was a new thing altogether.

The outlaws boarded the express car. They got about three thousand dollars from the safe. The gang got several hundred dollars and a quantity of jewelry from the passengers.

Twelve hours later, an express train carrying seventy-five thousand dollars in gold passed safely eastward over the re-placed rail. The advance agents of the outlaw band had made a miscalculation in time.

The gang mounted their horses and set their faces southward. Back for poor old Missouri, where, in spite of everything, it felt like home!

News of this outrage was published through the land, and even in Europe. If news is the unusual, then, truly, this was news. It was not merely unusual, it was unique.

The outlaws had started something new.

Throughout the Serious Seventies, many Pinkerton detectives hunted the James gang. The famous agency founded before the Civil War, by Allan Pinkerton, devoted much time and talent to capturing or killing the Jameses, the Youngers and their accomplices in outlawry.

From their headquarters in Chicago and from branch offices as well, the most astute operatives in the service were sent out after the bandits. Some never returned. It was the most memo-rable manhunt in American annals.

Before 1874 ended, John Younger died, with two Pinkerton detectives. Jim Younger got away.

Young Witcher, regarded as one of the most astute of the Chicago operatives, had requested that he be assigned the task of snaring the lions in their lair. He outlined his plan; the Pinkerton executives approved it. The considerable error com-mitted by the unfortunate young detective lay in his assumption that Frank and Jesse James were, after all, just a couple of rural bad men of average mental caliber, and that he could fool them with comparative ease.

Witcher went first to Liberty, the county seat, where he visited the Commercial Bank and made a cash deposit. He had a talk with the president of the bank, to whom he stated his intended plan to entrap the outlaws.

"Young man," advised the banker, "you'd better not try it. It won't be safe for you. You don't know those James boys as we know them, here in Clay County."

"Oh, I guess I'll try it, nevertheless," said Witcher, smilingly.

Then the detective called upon Col. O. P. Moss, a former sheriff of the county, and revealed his identity and his intentions.

"Mr. Witcher," the ex-sheriff warned him, "you don't know at all what you're going up against. I do. I know the resources of those James boys; they are not in any sense to be looked upon as ordinary criminals. You are not going out after a pair of city crooks, mind you. No—you are about to undertake the capture of two of the keenest-minded young men in America. Those boys are not asleep, I warn you! They never sleep, in the sense of being confident of security. If they happen to be at home, either of them, your life won't be worth fifteen cents if you go out there disguised as a farmhand—they'll see clean through you. I'm telling you, you can't fool Frank or Jesse James."

Nevertheless, young Witcher thought he could. Proceeding to the local hotel, he exchanged his city clothes for the outfit of a farm laborer. With a Smith and Wesson revolver concealed on his bosom, he took the afternoon train for Kearney, ten miles from Liberty, and about four miles from the Samuel homestead.

In the meantime, the Pinkerton man had been shadowed by a very private detective who lived in Clay County and was a particular friend of the Jameses. This unofficial sleuth mounted a swift horse and rode to the Samuel farm, where Jesse James was visiting his mother. He told Jesse all about the young stranger who was using such open-work detective methods.

Leaving the train at Kearney, Witcher walked out the road toward the farm. It was late in the afternoon, almost dusk, when, suddenly, he was challenged by a man who stepped out of the bushes with a big six-shooter in his right hand.

"Who are you, and where are you bound for?"

"I'm out looking for work on a farm," Witcher replied. "Can you tell me where I might be able to find a job in these parts?"

"You don't want any job—you've got one already, with that damn Pinkerton outfit," said the man with the drawn weapon, smiling sardonically.

"I don't know what you're talking about," the detective said. "I'm a poor man out of work, and—"

"And you're looking for the James boys, hey? Well, here, take a look at one of 'em—Jesse James!"

Witcher winced, but kept up his pretense. Jesse James signaled. Two other men stepped into the road.

"Search him," Jesse ordered.

One of the men extracted Witcher's weapon from its place of concealment. Jesse's eyes blinked angrily.

"A farmhand—with a loaded weapon on his chest!" he snarled. "Let me see your hands."

Jesse felt one of Witcher's palms—soft and smooth.

"A hell of a farm laborer you are! A poor man, hey? You put some of Mr. Pinkerton's money in the bank at Liberty, didn't you? And you left your fine clothes at the hotel. Where are you from—Chicago?"

"I'm from Indiana," responded Witcher, who was a native of the Hoosier state.

"Now I can't see why you don't let me pass on, for I'm not trying to harm you or anybody."

The three men consulted briefly.

"Better finish him, right here," suggested one.

Witcher began to plead for his life. He told his captors that he had a young wife at home, and for her sake he begged them not to kill him. Jesse James, who was going to take a young wife himself within a few weeks, is said to have been touched by this method of appeal.

Such was the statement made by members of his gang about

eight years later, whose confessions provide the raw material for this record of the meeting on the road out of Kearney.

"Well, don't let's do it here, anyhow—not on my side,"* Jesse is supposed to have said.

Late that night, the elderly man who operated the ferry at Blue Mills was awakened by some men on horseback; the hour was about 2:00 A.M. The party wanted to be ferried across the Missouri. The ferryman noticed that one of the four men was bound, hands tied behind him, feet secured by a cord under the horse's belly.

"Who's this fellow—why's he tied up this way?"

"He's a horsethief; we're out after a gang of 'em and just caught one."

The old ferryman then spoke directly to the bound man, who made no reply, though he gave his questioner an appealing look in the dim flare of the lantern.

"Gagged, by golly!" exclaimed the ferryman. "You-all must be afeared this here hossthief'll holler and skeer your hosses."

The party was ferried across.

A man about thirty years of age was shot to death and left lying in the road, across the Missouri River. He was dressed roughly, like a farmhand, but his hands were soft and smooth.

But the old jeans, pants, and coat, the old blue-check shirt, the old slouch hat—why such apparel? And just above the wrist, the initials "J. W. W." were found neatly tattooed.

---

*"My side" meant the Clay County side of the Missouri River.

8

The Little Rock express train from Saint Louis was due to come through Gadshill at 5:40 P.M., but not due to stop there. Shortly before the train was due to whiz past the little station, six men walked up to the depot, captured the station agent, and planted a signal flag in the middle of the track. Another turned the switch, which would compel the engineer to stop the train, even if he failed to heed the flag. The express train came along on time. The engineer obeyed the signal. This happened on January 31, 1874. The place was a lonely outpost in the foothills of the Ozarks, on the Iron Mountain Railroad.

When the conductor stepped to the ground alongside the station, lantern in hand, the first thing he saw was the muzzle of a pistol pointing at his head. Engineer and fireman were ordered to walk out into the woods, one of the robbers following them, pistol in hand.

Some of the robbers entered the Pullman sleepers and day coaches, compelling passengers to surrender valuables estimated to total about two thousand dollars. The express car was saved for last. More than a thousand dollars was taken from the safe. Mail bags were cut open; and a registered letter, containing two thousand dollars in cash, was later reported missing.

All the bandits wore masks of calico with eye-holes cut. The loot having been obtained, the train crew was told to pull ahead for Little Rock. The engineer yanked open his throttle, and the wheels began turning.

"Hey, you, hold up a minute!" cried one of the robbers waving his six-shooter.

The engineer stopped the train, expecting to be shot.

"Don't worry," called the robber. "I just wanted to get my overcoat off the track before you run over it."

*   *   *

55

Jesse James was in his twenty-seventh year when he married Miss Zerelda Mimms, his first cousin, who was of about the same age. The courtship was unusually long, almost nine years, and was carried on under difficulties sufficiently obvious as to make further explanation unnecessary. When the wounded young guerrilla was brought home from Nebraska, early in August, 1865, he was carried on a stretcher from a Missouri River steamboat to the home of John Mimms, at Harlem, now North Kansas City. Mimms had married a sister of the Reverend Robert James. The elder daughter of the Mimmses was the wife of Charles McBride, a well-to-do builder of houses in Kansas City. It was late in October before the patient was able to be taken, by wagon, from Harlem to the old homestead near Kearney. Relatives have stated that Jesse and Zerelda, before he left the Mimms home, entered into a compact to be married if Jesse ever recovered from his wound. Many months afterward, when at last he was able to get around outside the house, Jesse said to Mrs. Samuel:

"Ma, Zee and I are going to be married."

But the wedding was deferred from year to year, until the day when Jesse, dressed spic-and-span, mounted a handsome horse and, carrying a Winchester rifle across his saddlehorn, rode through Kearney's street on the way to his wedding. Beneath his coat were two Colt .45s.

On April 24, 1874, they were married at the home of a friendly neighbor near Kearney. The bride of Jesse James was a handsome blonde. He looked unusually happy.

"Congratulations, Jess," called out one who was on the friendship list. "Long life and prosperity!"

"Thank you, Sam," replied the bridegroom. "Come and see us—after we get settled down." But, for the young James couple, that time would never come.

* * *

Some months prior to the Witcher tragedy, another, wiser Pinkerton man had appeared in the Jesse James neighborhood. This fellow called himself Jack Ladd, and hired out as a farmhand to Daniel Askew, who operated a large farm near the Jameses. On Sundays, he donned his best clothes, a cheap hand-me-down suit, and went to church with the Askew family. He took part in the neighborhood social affairs. He became acquainted with Dr. and Mrs. Samuel and, to a limited degree, with Frank and Jesse James. (It was only at long intervals that the boys could visit their Mother, to whom they were deeply devoted.)

Jack Ladd was not suspected by the Jameses or by any of their friends of being anything other than an ordinary farm-hand—old Dan Askew's hired man.

In one month the Pinkertons had lost three men, but only one of the outlaws, John Younger, had been killed. On the afternoon of the twenty-fifth of January, 1875, it was reported by Pinkerton spies that Frank and Jesse James had been seen, since noon, in the yard of the old home.

That night, the Pinkerton operatives, accompanied by several men supposed to have been residents of Clay or Jackson, surrounded the Samuel farmhouse, arriving about midnight. All the occupants of the house were in bed, asleep. Neither Frank nor Jesse was there. With Dr. and Mrs. Samuel were the three Samuel children, an old Negro woman, and a small Negro boy. Archie Payton Samuel, half-brother to the James boys, was just eight and a half years old, the baby of the family.

Four men approached the house, each bearing a big ball of cotton waste soaked with kerosene and turpentine. They forced open the shutter of a kitchen window and were raising the sash when the old Black "aunty," sleeping in that room, was aroused by the noise. She gave a shrill shriek, awakening the whole family.

One of the men outside tossed one of the balls, which he had ignited with a match, through the window. The highly inflammable fluids caused it to burn brightly, lighting up the large room.

The entire family rushed into the kitchen. Dr. Samuel and his wife picked up tobacco sticks and began rolling the blazing ball toward the hearth, in an attempt to contain the fire within the fireplace, before the house was aflame.

Suddenly, through the window, came another ball of similar size and appearance. Although it was covered with burning cotton like the first, the second fireball was actually a bombshell, thrown into the room while the fire was still blazing. It was light enough in the room for any person within thirty yards to distinguish the faces, and the detectives were not thirty feet distant. The shell exploded, mangling Mrs. Samuel's right forearm. In the young boy's left side, a piece of the bomb had torn a frightful hole, through which his lifeblood was gushing—Archie died before dawn, after suffering most frightful agony. The Negro woman had aided Dr. Samuel, before the neighbors called in other surgical aid, in staunching the flow of blood from Mrs. Samuel's arm, which had to be amputated. The little Negro boy also had suffered a wound, from a fragment of the shell.

At dawn, one of the neighbors picked up, just outside the house, a large revolver, on the handle of which were carved the initials "P. G. G."—"Pinkerton's Government Guard."

Clay County people called the bomb-throwing episode "the crime of the century." Newspaper comment on the affair was not complimentary to the Pinkerton agency. In fact, editors throughout the United States vied with each other in expressing the utmost condemnation of the men who were "guilty of the inexcusable deed."

That January night was the seat of a tragedy that shocked the sensibilities of millions of people who read about it in the newspapers, and incidentally, made many new friends for the hunted James boys.*

Defeat of the amnesty bill was followed, after a quiet interval of about a month, by another tragedy in Clay County. This was the assassination of Daniel Askew, in whose employ the Pinkerton operative known as Jack Ladd had worked as a

---

*The writer of this true tale of blood and terror met Mrs. Zerelda Samuel at her home, many years after she lost her right arm and her youngest child. (Dr. Samuel had gone to his long rest, after a life of turmoil and trouble.) The aged widow, extending her left hand in greeting, impressed her visitor as a notably pathetic example of man's inhumanity to woman.

farmhand. The general public suspected the Jameses of having killed or instigated the killing of Farmer Askew as a matter of vengeance, and the tide turned against them.

On the evening of April 12, at about eight o'clock, Askew emerged from his house and went to a spring 150 yards away, to fetch a bucket of water. It was a moonlit night.

Askew returned to the house, set the bucket on a shelf on the porch, and dipped out a cup of water. As he was lifting the cup to his lips, the crack of rifle fire was heard. The farmer received three wounds, one bullet penetrating his brain. The assassins, local tradition has it, were hidden behind a woodpile.

There is a tradition that, a few minutes after this assassination, a citizen passing along a road not far from the Askew farmhouse met three armed men whom he recognized as the two Jameses and Clell Miller, and that one of the former announced:

"We've just been over and killed old Dan Askew, because he was in cahoots with those damn Pinkertons who threw the bombshell into our house."

9

The twelfth of May, 1875, five masked men stopped the stage bound for "San Antone," at a point about twenty-three miles southwest of Austin. Eleven passengers, three of whom were women, were aboard. The big coach was drawn by four horses.

Two of the holdup men took up position on one side of the coach, two, on the other, and the fifth, at the horses' heads. The driver and his passengers alighted under cover of six-shooters and lined up beside the coach. Two of the robbers passed along in front of the line, one holding open the mouth of a wheat sack. The other dropped purses, watches, and other personal articles of value into the capacious maw, as each victim contributed. This receptacle seemed grotesquely large for the limited loot, but, when the free-booters opened two or three trunks belonging to passengers, and extracted other valuables from their contents, and also cut open the mailbag and added a bundle of registered letters to the growing plunder, the sack turned out to be no bigger than its uses required.

The bandits were polite, the presence of the ladies apparently keeping their language genteel. They were also, it appears from the more or less hazy record, facetious fellows.

One of the travelers was Bishop Gregg of the Protestant Episcopal church in Austin. The bishop did not seem at first to comprehend the situation.

"You must give up your watch and your money, parson," said one of the robbers.

"What—do you mean to *rob* us?" inquired the bishop.

The robber laughed.

"We mean to *relieve* you of your surplus funds and your useless jewelry. You can call it robbery if you look at it that way, but we hardly care to apply so harsh a term to our business."

The bishop finally understood.

"I am a minister of the gospel," he told his adversary, "and I beg you to permit me to keep my watch; it is a present from an old friend."

"I recognized your calling, from your cloth," said the robber. "And we don't really like to compel a parson to do our bidding. But as to your watch, you really don't need it; your Master, the Nazarene, never owned one. And, as the Good Book commands you, when traveling, to take along neither purse nor scrip, we propose to put you in good standing with the Lord. Therefore, parson, shell out!"

Bishop Gregg give up cash and timepiece. Another passenger was a noted banker and capitalist of San Antonio. He was George W. Brackenridge, president of the First National Bank. Brackenridge surrendered watch and wallet.

Outlaw income from this robbery, including personal property and money and the cash taken from registered mail, was estimated at a total of approximately three thousand dollars.

The highwaymen also cut loose the lead team of horses and took the animals along when they mounted their own steeds and galloped away. The stage was many hours late when it pulled into San Antonio, about eighteen hours after the holdup, and the two horses that did double duty were well-nigh worn out. It was not until the stage reached the city that news of the robbery could be sent out.

In those times, it was the common fashion to accuse the Missouri outlaws of being guilty of almost every act of outlawry that took place anywhere within the area of a dozen states.

Bud McDaniels was a resident of Kansas City, working intermittently as a railroad switchman. He was not noted for anything resembling respectability. Through some mysterious source, McDaniels was supposed to have learned that a shipment of gold dust, from the Colorado mines, was to be aboard the express car of the train that left Denver on December 12, at 4:45 P.M. The next day, the train was stopped about a mile east of Muncie, railroad ties having been piled up on the track.

Six masked men carried out the affair in familiar border-bandit fashion. They uncoupled the express car and compelled the engineer to pull it a short distance from the beheaded train. The loot in this instance was richer than usual. The virgin gold and the coin and currency mounted well into a five-figure total. Some jewelry also was taken from the express car, which turned out to be unlucky for McDaniels.

Bud McDaniels couldn't stand his prosperity. He had a lady-love in Kansas City, to whom he boasted that he had come into possession of a fortune. Three days after the holdup, Bud hired a horse and buggy at a livery stable and called at his girl's home to take her out for a romantic ride. But his girl cut him for another fellow, just when he had acquired the cash to show her all sorts of good times. Bud drove his rig to a saloon, then to another, and yet another, and by nightfall he was drunk. He soon began to drive rapidly and recklessly. Police arrested him as he was whipping his horse through one of the downtown streets.

Before the police put him into a cell to sleep off his drunk, they searched him. He had more than a thousand dollars in cash, two large six-shooters, and some pieces of jewelry identified as a part of the plunder from the express car at Muncie. McDaniels said he had bought it to give to his girl.

"But she's gone back on me," complained Bud, "and I don't care who gets the jewelry now. I've got no use for such trash."

Investigation showed that Bud was out of town at the time of the train holdup. He was taken to Kansas. After preliminary hearing he was placed in jail at Lawrence. The grand jury indicted him for alleged complicity in the train robbery, but he escaped from a deputy sheriff who was taking him to the court-house for trial.

About a week later, Bud McDaniels was shot to death, near the Kaw river, by officers who recognized him and whom he resisted. He refused to give any information as to the identity of the robbers.

Now enters into the epic tale another McDaniels, brother to Bud. This was Thompson McDaniels, known as Tom. He was also presently to make tragic exit. Nearly a year after the Muncie affair, the Missourians transferred their activities to the

Middle East. Up to that time, daylight bank robbery had been confined to the Middle West. Now the industry assumed to have been invented by the one-time guerrillas of the border found itself transported to West Virginia for one day's operation. Huntington was the town chosen.

If any of the Missourians were on hand there, they were a long way from home. Four men rode into Huntington on September 1, 1875, and drew rein in front of the bank. Two dismounted and went inside. The others remained in their saddles and began firing pistol shots into the air to clear the streets.

Cashier Robert T. Oney opened the bank safe when ordered to do so. One robber kept him and a citizen who happened to be present under menace of a cocked weapon. The other collected several thousand dollars from the safe and cash drawer.

They rushed out, whistling shrilly for their accomplices, who brought up the two horses on leads. The bandits fired a few more shots as they dashed out into the country.

The pursuit following this raid was one of the most exciting in the records of American manhunting. Twenty men, well armed and well mounted, rode out from Huntington on the trail. From several other points, posses joined in the chase. When one posse lost the trail, another found it. There were several pistol fights with the fugitives, who found things so hot that they abandoned their horses more than once, stealing new mounts wherever they found available horseflesh. Their general route was to the southwest, through the mountains of West Virginia and eastern Kentucky.

About ten days after the robbery, two young farmers, brothers named Dillon, living in the Pine Hill of the Kentucky mountain region, read newspaper accounts of the chase and found reason to believe that the bandits were headed straight in their direction. The Dillons oiled and polished two old army muskets, which they loaded with slugs. They kept close watch out on the roads and trails near their home.

One moonlit night, two weeks after the bank raid, the Dillons saw four men stalking toward them through the woods. The handles of six-shooters were visible, sticking out from under the men's coats. The Kentucky mountaineers with the army muskets waited near the road. When the four strangers reached the road, they separated, two walking away from the hiding-place of the Dillons, two advancing in that direction.

"Halt! Throw down your pistols," the musketmen cried out as the two figures came near.

The strangers "threw down" their pistols by leveling them and firing at their challengers, who each fired one shot in return. The two strangers made off into the bushes. The Dillons went home.

10

The robbery of the Missouri Pacific train took place near Otterville, Cooper County, Missouri, on July 7, 1876. The train left Kansas City at 4:45 Friday afternoon, July 7, for Saint Louis. The train carried a combination express and baggage car, a smoker, several day coaches and two Pullman sleepers. All of the coaches were fairly well filled with passengers. At Sedalia, thirteen miles west of Otterville, the train took on an express car from the Missouri, Kansas and Texas, or "Katy" road, and it was coupled in, next to the express-baggage car. The Katy car was locked, with nobody riding in it. The baggage-master told the story this way:

It was a beautiful moonlit night, about 10 P.M. The train came to a stop near the western end of the wooden bridge across the Lamine river, a mile or so east of Otterville. This was in a place called Rocky Cut.

Pretty soon, three men climbed into my car. Bushnell, aware that a robbery was on the immediate program, went back in the train and handed the brakeman the key to his safe. The safe had no combination lock. When the robbers entered the car, they searched me for weapons and told me to stand over to one side, which I did. Their big guns didn't look nice. One of the robbers demanded that I give him the key to the safe. I told him I didn't have the key.

"Get it, then, and be quick about it, or you'll get hurt!" he said. At the same instant, he shoved the muzzle of his gun against my ribs. That gentleman, I think, was the renowned Jesse James.

"I'm only the baggagemaster," I explained.

"Where's the express messenger, then?"

"He's back in the train somewhere."

"Come with me and find him."

I went with him, for he still held his Colt in a threatening position. Bushnell was found, but he told the bandit he didn't have the key.

"Find it!" was the sharp order.

Bushnell was taken into the sleeper, where the brakeman sat.

Threatened with death, the brakeman handed over the key. The man with the big guns then marched us all back to the baggage car. The U.S. Express safe was opened with the key, and the money went into a wheat sack. The man who must have been Jesse James turned to the Adams Express safe.

"Here—where's the key to this?" he demanded, looking fiercely at Bushnell.

"I don't know," the messenger replied, explaining in detail that the safe was being shipped through, locked.

Finally the robbers seemed to conclude that he was telling them the truth, as, in fact, he was. Some of them got the fireman's coal hammer, or pick, brought it into the car, and tried to break the hinges of the safe door with the hammer, but failed. Then he gave the door several sharp, digging blows with the pointed end of the pick. This had little or no effect.

A bigger man, with a fist like a ham, seized the pick and dealt several blows. This man, from his size and strength, must have been Cole Younger. At last he made an opening in the safe, and this money also went into the wheat sack. It must have been Jesse James, asked me what was in the other express car. I explained that it was a car from the Katy and I didn't know what was in it.

He insisted that I unlock the car, so I did. We went in, and the robber looked about, satisfying himself that there was nothing that the gang could use to advantage.

The robbers now were about through with their work. One said, "You'd better go out and move some ties that we put on the track." Just as they were getting away, the leader called out:

"Well, if you see any of Allan Pinkerton's men, tell 'em they'd better come and catch us."

Their next raid was the most sensational and one of the most sanguinary in the world's annals of outlawry. The Otterville victory had provided them with plenty of ready money, nearly two thousand dollars apiece.

The First National Bank of Northfield, Minnesota, was to be the next. On the afternoon of Thursday, September 7, 1876, the gang rode into Northfield in three groups, having met for final consultation in a piece of woods about five miles out of town. At that meeting, each man was told precisely what part he was expected to take in the Northfield job.

Five of them visited that town on September 2, some putting up for the night at one hotel, and some at another.

Two or three called at the First National Bank, where one got change for a hundred-dollar bill.

A Mankato man who happened to know Jesse James "by sight," or so he averred, notified the police that the notorious Missourian was in their midst. But the local guardians of the people refused to believe that their modest hometown had been honored with a visit from such a celebrity. Jesse James was the last man they would expect to see there. The police were not impressed particularly with the probability that Jesse James was one of the visitors.

When the three robbers entered the bank, they found three employees. The robbers told the banker and his companions that the purpose of the invasion was to rob the bank.

"And don't any of you fellows holler!" he added. "We've got forty men outside, and it'll be no use to holler. It'll be dangerous if you do." Each robber had a revolver and his eye on a bank employee.

"I know you're the cashier," said one. "Now you open that safe, damn quick, or I'll blow your head off!"

The door of the vault, in which the safe was visible, stood open. Sam Wells rushed to the vault and stepped inside. The cashier arose and walked rapidly to the vault and tried to shut Wells inside. Before he could slam the heavy door shut, he was seized by both Wells and the leader of the robbing squad.

"Unless you open that safe at once, you'll be shot dead!" cried the leader.

"I can't open it—the time lock is on."

"You're lying!"

Repeatedly, they demanded that he open the safe, pulling him back and forth about the big room.

"Murder! Murder!" the cashier shouted. The leader struck him on the head with a heavy revolver, and he sank to the floor.

"Let's cut his damn throat!" cried Sam Wells, who opened his pocket knife and made a slight cut in the neck of the fallen man. The cashier lay on the floor near the vault, hardly conscious. Wells bent low and fired a shot close by the cashier's head—the first shot fired inside the bank. This was done in the hope of inducing him to unlock the safe. "There's money here, somewhere, outside the safe," he said. "Where do you keep it? Where's the cash till?"

On the counter was a box containing some fractional currency.* The teller pointed to this. Drawing from under his linen duster the inevitable wheat sack, Younger began to put the money into it—about three thousand dollars in paper money. And that was all the robbers got from the bank.

"Come out, boys! come out. They're killing all our men!" was the warning Wells and his two companions heard. The three escaped by way of the teller's window and the front door. The cashier got on his feet. He was groping his way toward his desk just as the last of the desperadoes, who was climbing through the teller's window, turned and shot the cashier. He dropped to the floor, dead.

Clell Miller died almost instantly. Tumbling from his saddle, he lay crumpled upon the ground. Bill Stiles was posted on sentry duty; his horse was at a standstill. The merchant's bullet went through the bandit's heart, and "Bill Chadwell" cashed in at last. Stiles's horse ran off to the livery stable.

Church bells had been set ringing. From all points in the little city, people were gathering in Bridge Square. Some were inspecting the corpses of Stiles and Miller. Still others were preparing to mount horses and pursue the six survivors.

Not far down the road from the point where Bob Younger found his mount, the six horsemen stopped in front of a farmhouse.

"We're deputies in pursuit of horse thieves," said a spokesman bandit, "and we want to borrow a saddle for this young man. He didn't have time to get his saddle when he joined us, and he's been thrown off and got his arm hurt."

---

*Paper money in denominations of less than one dollar, issued by the U.S. from 1863 to 1876.

The farmer cheerfully give them the loan of a saddle, but failed to kiss it farewell. Off again, on again, gone again—for Bob the Bandit.

Bob Younger certainly was having hard luck that day, despite his temporary pickup of horse and saddle. The impressed mount presently lost his ambition, stumbled, fell, and Younger's crushed elbow got another jolt. Younger was helped up behind a member of the band who was considerably lighter than Big Brother Cole.

Off again, on again, gone again! Some miles farther along, another farmhorse was commandeered. Bob got aboard and had high hopes again. But this beast balked so stubbornly that, after strenuous efforts to make him keep up with the cavalcade, he was mustered out, and, for the third time that dismal afternoon, Bob Younger had to ride double.

Thrice before nightfall, small squads of pursuers saw the fleeing robbers. Faribault, the seat of Rice County, having been notified by wire, sent out a posse.

The Faribault posse came within range of the robbers, and shots were exchanged. Everybody missed. The bandits galloped off into the woods. Hundreds of times had they done likewise when fighting under Quantrill. It was evident that they were making for the great forest region known as the Big Woods—swamps, lakes, rivers.

The scattered army of chasers included the chiefs of police from Minneapolis and St. Paul, private detectives, sheriffs, and many unofficial recruits. Some were on horseback, others on foot. Accordingly, men were posted at all bridges, fords, roads, trails and open places. This rim of pickets extended in a sort of semicircle for almost a hundred miles.

Six hundred, perhaps, after six! A hundred-to-one horserace and footrace chase! And the program continued, day and night, for two weeks, and all in the rain.

The swampy section of the Big Woods is a sorry place for foraging, even by such seasoned foragers as were these men, who had learned the art under Quantrill and Bill Anderson.

They had been on the retreat five days, and they were less

than fifty miles from Northfield. When the tied horse and the gnawed halters were discovered, the commanders of the chase felt seriously discouraged. Everybody had been looking for a bunch of men on horseback, nobody for anybody on foot. There were plenty of posses afoot, out looking for the robbers. Very likely, the Missourians had made themselves look like Minnesotans in pursuit of the invaders. Now they had three days' start, from the horse-tying camp.

Richard Roberts was a gallant youth who stood guard at a picket-line post on the road near Lake Crystal. Tired of standing by the roadside, someone said to Roberts, "What's the use to keep up this job? It's a farce! Why, everybody'll laugh at us when we get home."

"All the same, fellows," said Dick, "I'll keep it up; that's what they put me here to do."

"Little Dicky Bobby, Sunday-school boy!" taunted one of the derelict guards. "Say your prayers, Dicky, before you go to sleep tonight."

"You go to hell!" snapped little Dicky Bobby. It was a lonesome sentry job, there in the pouring rain; Dick himself didn't fancy it.

Ten days after the Northfield raid, there was a bitter quarrel, and the James boys cut loose from the crew. When they met people, they had a tale ready. They were officers chasing the James boys, and their horses and saddles had been stolen when they tied up to go into a restaurant to eat. Of course, a civic-spirited citizen "loaned" them horses and saddles, and other Minnesotans supplied them with food and refreshments. The James boys rode away on gray horses and saddles, but, by the time they reached the edge of Dakota Territory, the two grays were about worn out.

That night, in the dark, they found two black horses in a farmlot. They left the grays and rode away on the blacks. The new horses turned out to be stumblers. When daylight came, Jesse said to Frank, "Gosh a'mighty, Frank—this beast is blind in the left eye!"

"Shucks, Jesse—that's nothing at all to kick about; this one is blind in both eyes!" And they turned southward into what is now South Dakota, leaving Minnesota behind them.

Frank and Jesse exchanged the blind blacks for a second pair of grays that could see far and travel fast. They traveled into Iowa, by a dim trail, and eastern Nebraska for some distance, then traveled by train to some point near home.

One of the divertissements most richly enjoyed by Jesse, throughout his career as a hunted outlaw, was that of pretending to be an officer on his own trail. This helped him to elude the real officers, and Jesse had the joy of the joke to boot.

Just a week after the chase was centered on the Jameses, another big cartridge of news popped wide open in southern Minnesota. The other four had not escaped from the state, after all! They had been seen in the vicinity of the small village of Madelia, in the northeast corner of Watonwan County. The name of this place has come down to history in tragic association with the well-known Missouri surname Younger. They turned back and made for a bushy region in the river bottom.

Groups of manhunters gathered on both sides of the river, and the robbers were driven to bay. Sam Wells lay dead, five bullets having marked him. The three Youngers were captured, they too having been wounded. A wagon was brought forward. The corpse and the three Youngers were lifted into the bed of the vehicle.

"Drive to Madelia," was the sheriff's instruction. They turned about and accompanied the wagon to the Flanders House, where Cole Younger again became a guest of the landlord who had helped to capture him. The three brothers were put to bed, and surgeons called in to dress their many wounds. Their torn and blood-stained garments were ripped off, clean clothing was put on them, and food given them.

From the Twin Cities of Minnesota, and from other large cities in the northern Mississippi Valley, came newspaper photographers and reporters. Detectives, including a Pinkerton or two, visited Madelia to make sure that these were the Younger brothers.

When asked who they were, the three requested permission for a brief conference in private. This was granted, and then they told their names.

"And who's the dead man?" detectives inquired.

"We refuse to say, gentlemen," Cole Younger replied.

"The two members of your party killed at Northfield—who were they?"

"Again, we refuse to say."

"Well, then, tell us who the men are that got away—the other two; won't you?"

"We have agreed not to tell that, gentlemen."

"They are Frank and Jesse James; are they not?"

"They are not the Jameses," answered Cole Younger, "but, further than that, we shall say nothing."

Nor ever, to the day of either of their deaths, did either of the Youngers give anybody the name of any of their five companions. But Chief of Police James McDonough, of Saint Louis, and other police officials and detectives visited Northfield and Madelia, bringing means of definite identification of the three slain bandits, Stiles, Miller, and Wells. Within a few weeks the prisoners were able to walk about in their cells. On the ninth of November, they were shackled together and escorted under guard to the county courthouse for trial.

Judge Lord sentenced the three Youngers to imprisonment for life in the state prison at Stillwater. Robert Younger served out his time; he died in prison September 16, 1889. His prison deportment had been perfect. He was buried beside his mother in the family plot in the cemetery at Lee's Summit, Missouri, the old home town.

Coleman and James Younger—well, that's a different sort of story, and a most remarkable one, to be told later in this chronicle.

11

Almost exactly a year after the Northfield raid and its tragic results, a group of men rode into the county seat of Ogallala, in Keith County, Nebraska, far out on the plains.

The horsemen were seven. They told citizens of Ogallala that they were stockmen who had ridden up from Texas, disposing of a bunch of cattle on the way. They might buy a new bunch of steers, they said. These men, all of whom were garbed in frontier-cowboy fashion, made camp not far outside of town. Two of them visited the general store of F. M. Leech, in Ogallala.

"Why, hello, Jim!" Leech called out.

"Hello yourself; didn't know you were keeping this outfit."

"Yes, I'm the boss," replied Leech, "but I never expected to see Jim Berry out here. Where-all have you been, Jim, lately?"

"Oh, just cruising around. Been up to the Black Hills, for one place, and got me a nice little bunch o' gold dust. Think maybe I'll feel rich enough pretty soon now to take a trip back to old Callaway. Wife and children still there, on the old farm."

"What you doing now, Jim?"

"I'm in the cow game."

Merchant Leech was not particularly glad to see James Berry, whom he had known up at Plattsmouth as "Bad Jim." He had not known, until Berry mentioned it, that his visitor's old home was in Callaway County, Missouri.

Berry bought six big red bandanna handkerchiefs from Leech. It was a purchase common to the plains country, yet in this instance it was loaded with dynamite.

Some miles west of Ogallala was a station called Big Springs, where the Union Pacific Railway trains in those days stopped for water. The seventeenth of September, 1877, the eastbound Pacific express train halted at the Big Springs tank. Seven men arose from the sun-scorched grass, some on one side of the train, and some on the other. All were masked with red bandannas. Each held a six-shooter in his right hand, and some held a weapon in each hand.

"Hands up, and step down, lively!" commanded one gruff voice.

The engineer and his fireman obeyed. For the time being, four men stood by to guard the engine crew. Some of them went through the day coaches and Pullman sleepers, one of them carrying a wheat sack. Each held a six-shooter ready for any bad business.

"Hand over whatever you've got!"

Men and women alike gave up whatever they had. Some of them even surrendered bunches of keys. All went into the wheat sack. In the meantime, some of the other bandits entered the express car and ordered the Wells Fargo messenger to open his safe. He complied. The contents were dumped into another wheat sack. Much of this was in gold coins.

"Take it away now!" the leader of the band sang out to the engineer. "Good night and good luck!"

The engineer took it away at a speed exceeding schedule, making up most of the lost time before he shut throttle at Ogallala. There, the news of the holdup was put on the wires. Towns east, west, north, and south were warned to look out for seven suspicious strangers.

"Must have been the James gang—what do you think?" suggested the operator.

"Who knows?" responded the conductor. "They've never operated this far west before, so far as I know, but that wheat-sack business makes it look like those Missouri fellows." Ogallala men were more than a trifle slow in starting pursuit. Nobody took the lead until early next morning.

"Them there cowboys're camping just out of town."

"Sure! Let's take a look."

Three or four citizens rode out to the camp. They were all there, the seven stockmen, just beginning to fry some bacon. They greeted their unexpected visitors with the common cordiality of the plainsman.

"Heard the news?" one of the Ogallalans asked.

"News? What news?" It was Jim Berry speaking. The rest of the campers seemed to show a mild interest.

"Why, men, the U. P. express was held up and robbed at Big Springs last night, and—"

"The devil it was!" ejaculated Berry. "Who-all done it?"

"Who knows?" The conductor's comment repeated! The James boys were mentioned by one of the Ogallala men as possible contenders for the doubtful honor.

"Oh, well, you can't never tell," Jim Berry said. "Started any chase yet?"

"Making ready to, right off."

"You'd better hurry," advised Jim Berry.

The citizens returned to town. "Shucks!" they reported. "Them cowboys didn't have nothing to do with it; they're too all-fired lazy and trifling."

Shortly before the belated posse was organized, Jim Berry came rambling along the street. He said to Leech: "I heard you were about to lead a chase after them train robbers. That right?"

"Sure is, and if I don't catch 'em, it won't be my fault."

"Maybe you might like to have me come along and help?"

"First-rate idea; come right along, Jim."

"Got to go back to camp first and let the boys know. Maybe some o' them'll join your posse, too." Leech waited an hour or so, then started forth without Berry.

"I told you so," said one of the men who had visited the camp that morning, "them fellers are too lazy to join any excitement."

K. R. Ross, a farmer in Cass County, Missouri, was a family friend of the Jameses and the Youngers—related by marriage to the Younger family. From time to time, the outlaws visited his home. He entertained them but, since he had nothing to do with them as a free-booting gang, he notified "the boys" that he'd much prefer they didn't come around his place any more:

> Well, the boys understood the situation and kept away from the Ross place. Ross said that one day a man called at his farm with a note carrying a request that Ross go to a certain place in

the woods. The note was signed "David Howard." Ross knew that "David Howard" was Jesse James. He went, and there he found Jesse James, lying on the ground with his coat folded under his head, a .45 pistol in each hand, and his arms a-crossed on his chest. Jesse told Ross he had been down in the Mississippi river-bottom swamps and sick.

"When I started back to Missouri," said Jesse to Ross, "I thought of everybody I might trust, and I figured I couldn't trust anybody but you. I have no money, and I'm very sick."

Jesse then opened his shirt and showed Ross where, in the spring of 1865, a Federal bullet had entered the right side of his chest, when he returned to Missouri to surrender at the end of the Civil War. The place of the wound was "all inflamed," as Ross described it.

"I need a horse, too," said Jesse.

Ross provided him with a horse, saddled and bridled, and forty dollars. Jesse mounted the animal, with assistance, and rode away. In less than a month, so Ross declared, he had returned the horse, saddle, and bridle and repaid the money. Jesse James was honest about what he owed.

*   *   *

"One day," says Sam Allender, "Frank James told me that on a certain occasion he and Jesse were traveling on horseback somewhere in northwestern Missouri." It was about noon, and they were hungry. They pulled off the main road and found a lone woman in charge of a small farmhouse. They asked her if she could supply them with something to eat:

At first the woman hesitated. The men displayed money and assured her they would be glad to pay for what they ate. She then proceeded to prepare such scant food as she had on hand. As she was making coffee and cooking eggs, the James crowd sat around the room. They noticed that she was weeping; tears were rolling down her cheeks. "Jesse," [said Frank in telling me the story] "was always tenderhearted—couldn't stand a woman's tears." He asked her why she was crying. She tried to smile it off and said that seeing us men around the house reminded her of the happy times when her husband was living and had other men now and then helping him do the farm work, and she was just thinking how sadly things had changed since his death, and that was what made her cry, so she said.

Jesse kept on asking questions. The woman said that she had several children at school, some miles down the road. There was a mortgage on her farm, she went on to say, for fourteen hundred dollars, and it was overdue, and this was the last day of grace.

"Aha!" said Jesse, "and so that's really what's making you cry—you're afraid you're going to lose your home. I see."

Yes, that was it, she admitted. That very afternoon, said the weeping widow, the man who held the mortgage was coming out from town to demand his money. He was a hardhearted old miser, she stated, and she didn't have a dollar to apply on the debt. The man would be sure to foreclose and turn her and her helpless little ones out.

"Huh!" said Jesse, "that so?" his eyes blinking fast and furiously. "Well, now ma'am, I don't know about that; I—well, now, I think maybe you won't lose your farm after all."

The widow looked rather puzzled. She put the food on the table and all the men sat down and turned to. After they finished eating, Jesse produced a sack and counted out on the table fourteen hundred dollars.

"Here, lady," said Jesse. "You take this money and pay off your mortgage."

The lady was amazed. "I can't ever pay you back," she said, "and so I won't borrow it."

"But it's no loan," said Jesse. "It's a gift."

The widow said she couldn't believe it was anything but a dream—things never happened that way—but Jesse assured her it was no dream; the money was good money and it was for her to use. Jesse then wrote out a form of receipt, which he had the woman to copy in her own handwriting. He put the original into his pocket, so his handwriting wouldn't get into other hands. Jesse instructed the woman to pay the mortgage-holder the fourteen hundred dollars and have him sign the receipt—in ink. He then handed her a handful of cash for her immediate needs.

Jesse asked the grateful widow to describe the man who held the mortgage. She did so, telling the kind of rig he drove and about what hour she expected him, and the road by which he would come out from town. They then bade her good day and mounted their horses. The widow was still weeping, but weeping for joy.

As Frank James told Sam Allender:

We rode some distance from the house and hid in the bushes beside the road, along where the mortgage man was supposed to come in his buggy. Presently we saw him driving toward the widow's house, and pretty soon driving back, looking prosperous. He was humming "Old Dan Tucker was a fine old feller" as he came opposite. We stepped out into the road, held him up, and recovered the fourteen hundred.

It wasn't long after that a train robbery in the old-time style took place in Missouri—and right in Jackson County, too.

Jesse James had resurrected himself and reorganized his band. The hand of Jesse showed unmistakably in each of several robberies. First came the affair at Glendale, a small station in Jackson County, on the Chicago and Alton Railroad, October 7, 1879. The express train was robbed by the James gang.

But the next train robbery, which resulted in two murders, was known as the Winston holdup. At the town of Winston, in Daviess County, July 15, 1881, a passenger train on the Chicago, Rock Island and Pacific Railroad was robbed. William Westfall, train conductor, and Frank McMillan, workman employed by the railway company, were shot to death, and the James gang rode away.

Third and last of this series, the final unlawful act committed by the Jesse James gang was the Blue Cut affair, in Jackson County, September 7, 1881, exactly five years after Northfield.

12

Two men, Charles and Robert Ford, had been occupying one of the rooms in the rear of the house where Jesse lived with his wife and family. Unknown to the Jameses, the Fords had had a secret compact to kill Jesse for some time—close to a year. In all those months they had been with Jesse, they were watching for an opportunity to shoot him. But he was always so heavily armed that it was impossible to draw a weapon without Mr. James seeing it.

The opportunity they had long wished for finally came one morning. Breakfast was over. Charlie Ford and Jesse James had been out to the stable currying the horses, preparatory to their night ride. On returning to the room where Robert Ford was, Jesse commented, "It's an awfully hot day."

He pulled off his coat and vest and tossed them on the bed. Then he said, "I guess I'll take off my pistols, for fear somebody will see them if I walk in the yard."

He unbuckled the belt in which he carried two .45 Colts and laid them on the bed with his coat and vest. He then picked up a dusting brush with the intention of dusting some pictures which hung on the wall.

His back was now turned to the brothers, who silently stepped between Jesse and his revolvers. Robert drew his gun to a level with the back of Jesse's head, not more than four feet from his back.

He made a motion as if to turn his head to see what the cause of that suspicious sound was, but too late. A nervous pressure on the trigger and the gun went off. Jesse James fell backward, on the floor in his own home.

The ball came out over the left eye. It had been fired out of a Colt .45, improved pattern, silver-mounted and pearl-handled pistol, presented by the dead man to his slayer only a few days ago.

Mrs. James had been in the kitchen when she heard the shot, and she dropped her household duties and ran into the front room.

She saw her husband lying on his back, his slayer Robert Ford holding his revolver in his hand, and making for the rear of the house. Mrs. James stepped to the door and called to him:

"Robert, you have done this! Come back!"

Robert answered, "I swear to God I didn't!"

The Fords then returned to where she stood. Mrs. James ran to her husband's side and lifted up his head.

Life was not yet extinct. She asked him if he was hurt— it seemed to her that he wanted to say something but could not. She tried to wash away the blood that was coursing over his face from the hole in his forehead, but it seemed to her that the blood came faster than she could wipe it away. Jesse James died in her arms.

Charlie Ford explained to Mrs. James that a pistol had "accidentally" gone off.

"Yes," said Mrs. James, "I guess it went off on purpose." The two boys left the house and went to the telegraph office, where they sent a message to Sheriff Timberlake of Clay County. Throughout the land, the news spread like wildfire.

The body was removed to an undertaking establishment two hours after the tragedy, Mrs. James accompanying it. She left her children, Jesse and Mary, six and a half and three, with the woman who lived next door and who had known "the Howards" as "very quiet people." "Mrs. James," according to a newspaper account, "was greatly affected by the tragedy, and her heartrending moans and expressions of grief were sorrowful evidence of the love she bore for the dead desperado."

At midnight, a special train to Kearney was furnished by officials of the Rock Island railroad. The train reached Kearney at 2:45 A.M. The baggage car carrying his corpse had been robbed nine years earlier by Jesse James.

At the inquest, after the identification of the corpse, Jesse's mother was instructed by the coroner to raise her right hand to be sworn. Mrs. Samuel lifted the stump of the forearm that had been blown off by the Pinkerton bomb in 1875. Virtually everybody present knew the tale of that tragic midwinter night. There was absolute silence in the chamber for a moment; then somebody, overcome by the compelling pathos of the incident, caught his breath and sobbed. The coroner's voice was husky as he proceeded:

"Mrs. Samuel, are you the mother of Jesse James?"

"I am—oh, my God!" she sobbed.

Her age, she said, was fifty-seven. Her son Jesse was midway in his thirty-fifth year. The corpse she had just viewed, she said, was that of her son. Then the widow of Jesse James testified that she was born in Kentucky, that she had been the wife of Jesse James for nearly eight years, and that her age was thirty-five.

"We came here," she said, "to live as other people do. They tell some hard things on my husband, but a better man never lived."

"Was Jesse a drinking man?" she was asked.

"No, sir. He never drank, smoked, nor chewed. He never liked whiskey. He never swore in my presence and he wouldn't allow others to do so."

Sheriff Timberlake of Clay County testified that he had known Jesse James from 1864 to 1870. He had not seen him since the latter date, but he recognized the corpse.

The body lay in a five-hundred-dollar coffin, furnished by Craig and Timberlake. After a fervent prayer by the Reverend Mr. Jones, the funeral sermon was preached by the Reverend J. M. P. Martin, pastor of the church. His text was Matthew 24: 44. In closing, Pastor Martin stated that Mrs. Samuel wished him to request that those present refrain from going out to the farm, where interment was to take place.

Jesse James was buried in a corner of the yard, on the premises where he was born, where his mother could look out from her window at the mound at the foot of a big coffee-bean tree. Mrs. Samuel planted flowers upon the grave, and, for twenty years, she tended them with affectionate care. A tall, white marble monument was erected there, on which Mrs. Samuel had this inscription engraved:

In Loving Remembrance of My Beloved Son
JESSE W. JAMES
Died April 3, 1882
Aged 34 Years, 6 Months, 28 Days
Murdered by a Traitor and Coward
Whose Name Is Not Worthy to Appear Here

And so, at last, the world's most hunted man—and, according to his friends, the most hounded—after nearly twenty years of warring and worrying, came home to rest, undisturbed, for another score of years.

EPILOGUE

Robert Ford, aged twenty, and Charles Ford, twenty-four, were found guilty of the murder of Jesse W. James and were sentenced to be hanged. Two hours after the court pronounced sentence, the wires carried news of the issuance of a pardon to each, from the governor of Missouri.

The reward of ten thousand dollars had not been offered for Jesse James "dead or alive." The executive who had offered it, therefore, had not "conspired" with the Ford boys for the assassination of Jesse James, and they got just a small part of the reward. Charlie Ford, in less than a year, shot himself to death in a weed patch near Richmond, Missouri.

Bob Ford went out to a mining town of Creede, Colorado, and opened a low bar and gambling den. A deputy sheriff named Ed Kelley led a raid on Ford's place, February, 1892. Ford was standing behind his bar one day when Kelly, who was no longer a deputy, entered the door armed with a double-barrel shotgun.

Ford's revolver was on a shelf behind him. He reached for it, but Kelly turned loose both barrels of his gun with buckshot, and Bob Ford died, suddenly and with his boots on. Some years after this, Kelly was killed in a gunfight in Texas.

There was a second burial of Jesse James, after twenty years, in 1902. The two grave-diggers worked about four hours in the heavy rain to open the grave in the corner of the yard. From under the old coffee-bean tree, and seven feet down, the remains of Jesse James were taken up and put in a handsome new casket covered in black, with a silver plate bearing the name "Jesse James," and buried in the cemetery,

Jesse James had a wife;
She was a mourner all her life;
And his children, they were brave.
Oh, the dirty little coward
That shot Mr. Howard!
And laid Jesse James in his grave.

And they "laid Jesse James in his grave," for the second and, doubtless, the last time, not as a bandit, but as a brother-in-arms, as a soldier, as a guerrilla rough rider of the border warfare, as a fighter in the lost cause, a squad of Quantrill's men who rode and shot with the boy Jesse James in the last two years of the Civil War.

*   *   *

On October 5, 1882, when Jesse James had been dead about six months, two well-dressed men, a Major Edwards and one Frank James, went to the office of Governor Crittenden. They were admitted by Finis Farr, the governor's secretary. Major Edwards shook hands with the governor.

"Governor," he said, "allow me to introduce my old friend—Frank James."

"I'm glad to meet you, Mr. James," said the governor, extending his hand.

"And I am glad to meet you, Governor," said Mr. James.

One of the politicians, sitting back against the wall about twenty feet away, gasped: "Good God! I can't believe it!"

Nevertheless, it was so. Frank James, cool, calm, collected, master of such emotions as he felt, opened his coat, revealing a thick leather belt crammed with cartridges and showing, at the middle, a big bronze buckle marked "U.S."

He unbuckled the belt and removed it. Attached to it was a holster from which protruded the gleaming handle of a big six-shooter, a Remington .44. Holding the belt in his left hand, and, with his right hand plucking the pistol from the holster and deftly moving his fingers down the polished barrel, he extended it, handle foremost, toward the governor of his native state.

"Governor Crittenden," said the elder and abler brother of the late Jesse James, "I want to hand over to you that which no living man except myself has been permitted to touch, since 1861, and to say that I am your prisoner. I have taken all the cartridges out of the weapon," he added, after a brief pause, "and you can handle it with safety."

A most dramatic event in the history of human civilization was happening before the astonished eyes of the governor's guests. Governor Crittenden accepted the belt and the six-shooter, handling the latter somewhat gingerly. He seemed surprised at the weight of the weapon.

"Not since 1861!" The governor's voice intoned surprise.

The governor had assured his correspondent—the communication having been sent to Mrs. Frank James and forwarded to her husband—that the state would guarantee him a fair trial in every respect.

The trial opened at Gallatin, capital of Daviess County, on August 21, 1883. It lasted eight days and took place in the Gallatin Opera House, because the courtroom was too small to accommodate all the people who were eager to witness the proceedings. The sheriff issued tickets of admission, not to exceed the seating capacity of the opera house. Thus, no "S. R. O." sign was displayed.

After being absent three and a half hours, the jury returned a verdict finding Frank James "Not guilty." But Frank was not free. He was taken back to Independence, to be put on trial for the Blue Cut train robbery. Dick Liddil was to be the witness for the state, but Liddil had done time for horse-stealing. Since a person that had been convicted of a crime was not competent to testify in a court, there was nothing left to do except dismiss the case. And thus ended the career of the other Missouri outlaw.